Pasta & Garlic

Low-Fat Recipes...That Work!

Chris Gluck

Illustrations by John Molenaar

Wine Selections by Edmund Osterland, MS

Pasta Press Publishing
San Diego, California

Grateful acknowledgment is made to the following pasta and garlic lovers, without whom this book would have been impossible.

The recipe on page 30 is reprinted by permission of Helene Siegel.

The recipe on page 32 is reprinted by permission of Michael Chiarello.

The recipes on pages 34 and 84 are reprinted by permission of Trattoria Acqua.

The recipes on pages 36, 38 and 76 are reprinted by permission of Jeanne Jones.

The recipes on pages 40, 60 and 64 are reprinted by permission of Hugh Carpenter and Ten Speed Press. They were adapted from *Hot Pasta* by Hugh Carpenter and Teri Sandison. Copyright © 1996 by Hugh Carpenter and Teri Sandison.

The recipe on page 48 is reprinted by permission of Arlyn Hackett.

The recipe on page 50 is reprinted by permission of Mark Carter.

The recipe on page 54 is reprinted by permission of Ingrid Croce.

The recipe on page 58 is reprinted by permission of Daniel McKenna.

The recipe on page 70 is reprinted by permission of Scott Fraser.

The recipe on page 72 is reprinted by permission of Cafe Pacifica.

The recipe on page 78 is reprinted by permission of Kitty Morse.

The recipe on page 80 is reprinted by permission of Henry Fenwick.

The recipe on page 82 is reprinted by permission of Habib Kolahi.

Pasta Press Publishing
Post Office Box 3070
San Diego, CA 92163

Publisher's Cataloging-in-Publication

Gluck, Chris.
     Pasta & garlic : low-fat recipes-- that work! / Chris Gluck ; illustrated by John Molenaar : wine selections by Edmund Osterland. -- 1st ed.
     p. cm.
     Includes bibliographical references and index.
     ISBN: 1-891004-01-8
     1. Low-fat diet--Recipes. 2. Cookery (Pasta) 3. Cookery (Garlic) I. Molenaar, John. II. Osterland, Edmund. III. Title. IV. Title: Pasta and garlic.

RM237.7.G58 1997   641.5'638
                                                        QBI97-40929

LCCN: 97-092294
Printed in USA
02 03 04 05 06 07 • 10 9 8 7 6 5 4 3

Dedicated To

Mary, Erica and Katie

*The three most important women in my life, and
the best pasta testers a husband and father could ask for!*

Table of

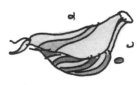

Contents

Dear Fellow Garlic Lover

As publisher of *Pasta Press* magazine, the part I like best about my job is eating pasta! Over the past several years, I've tasted, tested, re-tested, designed, re-designed, agonized over, given up on, worked on, re-worked, over-worked, been delighted with, overjoyed with and experienced sheer ecstasy with countless pasta recipes. Because our staff is so small *(but probably mostly because I'm a little overly passionate about recipe quality)*, I personally make every single recipe that gets printed—which means that we eat pasta every single day! Consequently, dinner time is usually "new recipe testing time," and, as a result, sometimes becomes a little tense during the first few minutes. (After all, how many people do you know who sit down to eat with a notepad next to their plate—and whose children know not to interrupt while mama and papa are "tasting?") If the recipe works it's cause for celebration; if not, it's make a few notes and back to the drawing board.

With all this pasta eating going on in our home, it didn't take long for us to notice that most of the recipes that worked shared a common ingredient—garlic! Then we noticed that the ones that *really* worked had something else in common. Not only did they contain garlic, they contained *lots* of it!

This book is a collection of those recipes. They were developed in conjunction with over a dozen of the finest chefs, cookbook authors and cooking instructors in America. So, whether you're a fellow garlic lover, or if it's just healthy, flavorful food that you're after, look no further! I'm sure you'll enjoy making these recipes as much as we enjoyed putting them together for you!

Introduction — How We Lost 20 Pounds Eating Pasta

It all started in April 1993. Our oldest daughter Erica (seven years old at the time) was so eager to earn her own spending money that she threatened to sell her Teddy bears on the sidewalk unless we could help her find a job. My wife, Mary, contacted several small businesses in our neighborhood on her behalf, but after being turned down for *any* type of employment, Erica realized that her only option was to start her own business. (Being self-employed all our lives, Mary and I certainly didn't want to quash any entrepreneurial tendencies in our first-born—although we did have a few reservations about her youth!)

For years we had purchased the most wonderful homemade fresh pasta from a small neighborhood shop that specialized in exotically flavored pastas. Erica reasoned, with typical child-like innocence, that if she liked it so much everyone else would, too. So it came as no surprise when she proposed the idea of selling flavored fresh pasta at our local farmers' market one night a week. More to encourage her than anything else, we half-heartedly decided to give it a try. We started with $100 in product inventory and a few borrowed card tables and coolers.

Quite frankly, we never expected this venture to be anything more than a glorified lemonade stand—and we certainly didn't expect it to last for more than a couple of weeks. Were we ever in for a big surprise! The business quickly exploded. Eventually we had to give up our "real" jobs just to keep up with it!

Our enthusiasm was short-lived, however. While initial demand had been extremely promising, sales began to decline as the novelty wore off. We learned the hard way that consumer awareness about flavored fresh pasta was practically non-existent. Many of our regular customers didn't know how to prepare it correctly, nor did they realize its enormous versatility.

So, we set out to educate our customers by putting together a simple one-page brochure, *Commonly Asked Questions About Flavored Fresh Pasta.* In it we shared some basic cooking techniques and explained how to create delicious and easy-to-prepare low-fat sauces. Response was enthusiastic and sales picked up again. Mission accomplished!

But it didn't stop there! After discovering how delicious pasta could really be, many of our now devoted regular customers encouraged us to print a new brochure with even more tips and recipes. Over the course of the following year, the one-page brochure evolved into a small, locally distributed newsletter; then into our internationally distributed quarterly magazine, *Pasta Press*; and ultimately this book.

That original brochure also explained how we effortlessly lost 20 pounds each by switching to a low-fat diet utilizing lots of pasta! This is an important point- and the one that ultimately brought about the magazine and then this book. You see, *our weight loss happened quite by accident.*

Like many Americans, we were struggling to lose those last few extra pounds. We'd go on a diet, lose them, get bored, go off the diet, and then gain them, and a few more, right back again. It seemed that no matter how hard we tried, we were doomed to failure. To make matters worse, every time we thought we had everything under control, our taste buds would stage their own little revolution, saying "We don't care how healthy this is! It tastes terrible and we're not going to eat it anymore!"

But what happened next was quite unexpected. One day about three months after starting the business, Mary and I realized that our clothes were fitting more loosely. This came as a real shock since one of the fringe benefits about working at a farmers' market is that there's never any shortage of food. As a result, and because we were never ones to push aside a plate, we found that we were eating larger and larger quantities of food. If anything, we should have expected to gain weight. Stepping on the scale however, confirmed our hopeful suspicions. *We had each lost 20 pounds— all while consuming greater quantities of food than ever before, and without offending our temperamental taste buds! Furthermore, we both had more energy than ever and, as another unexpected bonus, a subsequent check-up revealed that our cholesterol levels were in the 140's!*

Naturally ecstatic, we wanted to share the good news with everyone! So we threw ourselves into learning everything we could about how pasta related to healthful and delicious eating. Along the way we discovered overwhelming clinical evidence indicating that a diet low in fats, especially saturated fats, and high in complex carbohydrates and fiber will produce the welcome benefits we experienced. Since pasta is high in complex carbohydrates, and because our sauces had typically been spur-of-the-moment low-fat concoctions based largely on left-over produce from the farmers' markets, it gradually dawned on us that *we had unknowingly developed healthful eating habits!* In retrospect, what made it so easy was that the food tasted good—and there was plenty of it.

It didn't take us long to realize that our new high-complex carbohydrate, high-fiber, low-fat eating regimen had painlessly accomplished what a lifetime of deprivation-based dieting never would! So, if you're interested in losing weight or improving your health—or if you just want to sample some great new pasta dishes, I invite you to try the recipes that follow. They're all under 20% of calories from fat and I'm confident your taste buds will approve.

(Our favorite complement is, "How can this be low-fat? It tastes too good to be healthy!")

One final note: This is what worked for us and for countless others. However, I am not a doctor nor am I dispensing medical advice! Please check with your personal physician and do your own independent research before making any dietary, exercise or lifestyle changes!

To your good health and long life!

Why are the Recipes Under 20% of Calories from Fat?

Dieting...Without Going Hungry!

Ask any dieter why it's difficult to stick with most diets and the likely response will be one word—deprivation! Typically, most conventional weight loss diets are based on caloric restriction of some type, and most of us simply don't enjoy being restricted or deprived—especially when it comes to food! If we leave the table even the least bit hungry, that's a sure sign of temptations to come! And herein is where I believe the problem lies. Even though the average dieter will probably experience some degree of immediate weight loss on most diets, for many this may simply not be enough to combat the persistent hunger pangs typically associated with deprivation-based dieting. That's the bad news. Now here's the good news.

How Does Pasta Fit In?

Many studies (and our personal experiences) indicate that by implementing a low-fat, high-complex carbohydrate diet, weight loss may be achieved without deprivation. Although the USDA currently defines a low-fat diet as one that derives less than 30% of its calories from fat, many physicians and nutritionists recommend levels below 20%. This latter criteria is the one our family uses and the one that all of the recipes in this book follow.

If your objective is to make the switch to low-fat (under 20% of calories from fat) eating, pasta may be just what you're looking for! Because it is high in complex carbohydrates, and because the fat calories comprise less than 10% of total calories, by itself, pasta immediately satisfies the "under 20%" criteria. And, because it is an extremely versatile base to which you can add a multitude of your favorite ingredients, it can also be prepared in ways to satisfy just about everyone's "taste bud" criteria. Beware of rich sauces containing extravagant amounts of cheese, cream, butter and meats though! They can quickly push the overall percentage of calories from fat to unacceptably high levels!

But exactly what is it about eating low-fat, high-complex carbohydrate foods that enables most people to eat until they're satisfied—with apparent disregard to calorie counting? To illustrate let's first discuss the differences between calories.

Are All Calories Created Equal?

In a word, no! Calories from fat and calories from carbohydrates or protein differ in two very important ways. First, one gram of fat has over twice as many calories as an identical amount of either carbohydrates or protein. (1 gram of fat = 9 calories vs. 1 gram of carbohydrates or protein = 4 calories.) Second, it is much easier for our bodies to convert foods that are high in fat directly into body fat than it is to convert foods that are high in carbohydrates.

What does this mean? Because the body's ability to store complex carbohydrates like pasta is limited (unlike fat calories which have a tendency of going straight to our hips or belly!), even when people eat more complex carbohydrates than their bodies can absorb, these excess calories are more readily burned than excess calories from fat. Put another way, you will have to work much harder to burn off a high-fat cheeseburger than you will a low-fat serving of pasta—even though both may contain the identical amount of calories! Furthermore, the pasta portion will be much larger than the cheeseburger—meaning that you will most likely get filled up on fewer calories! This suggests that perhaps the *composition* of one's diet may be of great importance when it comes to gaining or losing weight.

Overeating High-Fat Foods is Easier

As a practical matter, it's much easier to overeat high-fat foods than it is low-fat foods. For example, did you know that a 1½ ounce portion of potato chips has the same amount of calories as a 10 ounce baked potato? Even though the *amount* of calories is identical, you'll probably still be hungry after eating the chips (and want to eat a lot more!) On the other hand, you'll probably feel full after eating the baked potato. But here's the real problem: The chips have over 14 grams of fat while the baked potato has less than ½ gram!

Here's another example. Compare the recipes in this book against a cheeseburger, fries and a shake—a typical fast food meal. The pasta recipes average around 465 calories, with calories from fat averaging less than 16%. However, depending on the restaurant, the fast food meal will average around 1,600 calories with almost 50% of those coming from fat. (Furthermore, most of the pasta recipe's fat is monounsaturated, or "good" fat, while much of the fast food meal's is saturated, artery clogging, "bad" fat.)

From strictly a caloric standpoint, you would have to eat over three main course servings of pasta to equal the number of calories in one fast food meal. Is it possible? Yes. Is it likely? Probably not.

But for the sake of argument, let's assume that you did "overeat" low-fat (less than 20% of calories from fat) complex carbohydrate foods like pasta. Would you gain weight? Maybe, maybe not. Let's take a look a recent study done at the University of Illinois at Chicago.

An Actual Case Study

In a well documented study (*American Journal of Clinical Nutrition, Vol. 54, pp. 304–310, 1991*) researchers from UIC performed a 24 week study on 18 overweight sedentary women. The subjects were fed a control diet of 37% fat (the average American's diet) for an initial 4 week period and then switched to a 20% fat diet. All other factors, including lack of exercise, were constantly monitored and remained stable throughout the study. After 20 weeks of lower-fat eating, the women lost an average of approximately 5 pounds each—*in spite of consuming significantly more (15–28%) calories than on the high-fat diets.*

Dr. Phyllis Bowen, one of the original researchers, told me that many of the women complained that they couldn't eat all of their food when the initial switch was made from high-fat to low-fat—*even though the calorie levels were the same!* It took them 1–2 weeks to adjust to the higher quantities of lower-fat food. Dr. Bowen went on to say that after this adjustment period, they had to gradually increase the quantity of food in an attempt to maintain body weight. ***Despite these efforts, the group as a whole continued to lose weight!***

But perhaps most importantly, everyone's *lean muscle mass percentage* increased while their body fat decreased. (Muscle weighs more than fat but takes up less volume. In addition to countless health benefits, a higher percentage of lean muscle mass usually translates to a more attractive physique. So by definition, in addition to just losing weight, these women were also reshaping. Dr. Bowen confirmed this, saying that even though the average weight loss was *only* five pounds, many of the women were ecstatic at being able to fit back into clothes they hadn't been able to wear in years!)

The Bottom Line

Whether you are interested in weight management, maintaining your health, or just great food, we have seen many benefits to a low-fat, yet savory eating regimen that includes lots of complex carbohydrates like pasta. Like they have for us, I hope these recipes help you achieve your weight and health goals. I think you'll be thrilled with the long term results!

Who's in the Kitchen?

Hugh Carpenter Hugh Carpenter is a writer and cookbook author. He also teaches at cooking schools throughout North America in addition to running his own culinary school in Napa Valley. Known for creative recipes with explosive flavors, his current "Hot" cookbook series (*Hot Wok, Hot Chicken, Hot Pasta, Hot Barbecue*, Ten Speed Press) is breaking all records.
- *Wild Mushroom Pasta (page 40)*
- *Pasta Marrakech with Chicken (page 60)*
- *Caribbean Pasta with Chicken (page 64)*

Mark Carter Mark Carter and his wife Christi built, own and operate Carter House Inn, Hotel Carter and Restaurant 301 in the rugged northern California seacoast town of Eureka. Located in the middle of the giant redwoods, and considered a "destination" by many, the restaurant boasts site-grown organic produce, regional specialties and a wine list with over 1,500 vintages.
- *Pasta with Roasted Chicken & Mushrooms (page 50)*

Michael Chiarello Michael Chiarello is the chef/proprietor of *Tra Vigne* in Napa Valley, and several other restaurants in California and Colorado. He is a partner in *Napa Valley Kitchens*, a specialty foods production and marketing company that distributes his *Consorzio* line of flavored olive oils and vinegars, as well as other items. He is also author of *Flavored Oils* and *Flavored Vinegars* (Chronicle Books).
- *Penne with Caramelized Shiitakes & Asparagus (page 32)*

Ingrid Croce Ingrid Croce is a cookbook author (*Thyme in a Bottle*, Harper Collins) and chef/proprietor of *Ingrid's Cantina* and *Croce's Restaurant and Jazz Bar*, her tribute to her late husband, singer-songwriter Jim Croce. Her restaurants are located in San Diego's historic Gaslamp district and feature contemporary American cuisine with live jazz nightly.
- *Pasta with Grilled Eggplant & Chicken (page 54)*

Scott Fraser Scott Fraser is the chef at *Kasteel Franssen*, located in Whidbey Island, Washington. He received his formal training in the traditional French cooking school, Pierre Dubrulle in Vancouver, British Columbia. Known for his heart-healthy gourmet preparations, Fraser blends local Northwest cuisine with his French cooking skills.

- *Spicy Singapore Prawns (page 70)*

Chris Gluck Chris Gluck is a cooking instructor, the author of *Pasta & Garlic* and the owner, publisher and editor of *Pasta Press*, a quarterly magazine featuring delicious, low-fat pasta recipes. His mission is to show everyone that, with pasta, it's easy to eat delicious and healthy food at the same time.

- *Garlic & Basil "Raw" Sauce (page 26)*
- *Three Variations on a Squash Stir-Fry (page 28)*
- *Fried Gnocchi in Tomato Basil Cream Sauce (page 44)*
- *Grilled Chicken with Roasted Tomato Cream (page 56)*
- *Gnocchi with Italian "Sausage" & Tomatoes (page 62)*
- *Pasta with Seared Scallops (page 68)*
- *Pasta with Mussels & Garlic in White Wine (page 74)*
- *Spaghetti with Garlic & Wilted Spinach (page 80)*

Erica Gluck Erica Gluck is an aspiring juvenile chef and the author of *Beyond Macaroni & Cheese*, a children's cooking column in *Pasta Press* magazine. Not unlike her father, her mission is to show children (and parents) that the likelihood of living a healthy, vibrant, disease-free existence as an adult is much better if healthy eating habits are established at a young age.

- *Burnt Carrot Soup (page 42)*
- *Easy Chili Pasta (page 52)*

Arlyn Hackett Arlyn Hackett is a cooking instructor and the consulting editor of *Pasta Press*. He served as the executive chef at *Pritikin Longevity Center* for seven years and was also the star of the PBS television cooking series, *Health Smart Gourmet Cooking*. He has written several low-fat cookbooks, including his latest, *Arlyn Hackett's Menu Magic* (Hastings House).

- *Salsa Veracruz with Chicken & Pasta (page 48)*

19

Jeanne Jones Often called the "Dear Abby" of the food section, Jeanne Jones is the internationally syndicated columnist of *Cook It Light.* She is also the author of numerous cookbooks, including her latest, *Healthy Cooking for People Who Don't Have Time to Cook* (Rodale Press). With her message of common sense and moderation, she speaks directly to the health concerns and trends of today, proving once again that eating well does not mean sacrificing the pleasures and enjoyment of food.

- *Pasta with Fresh Vegetables & Basil (page 36)*
- *Stir-Fried Ginger & Garlic Noodles (page 38)*
- *Chinese Pasta with Bay Scallops (page 76)*

Habib Kolahi Habib Kolahi is the executive chef of Iguana Cantina in Waltham, Massachusetts. He received his culinary experience while working at several Boston area restaurants.

- *Pasta with Flambéed Shrimp (page 82)*

Daniel McKenna Daniel McKenna received his formal training at the California Culinary Academy and his culinary experience while working at several San Francisco and southern California restaurants and hotels. He was voted Rising Star Chef of the Year by the San Francisco Chronicle in 1995.

- *Penne with Smoked Chicken Sausage (page 58)*

Kitty Morse Born in Casablanca, Kitty Morse emigrated to the United States in 1964. With her repertoire of family recipes, she began catering Moroccan parties, which in turn led to teaching Moroccan and Mediterranean cooking classes. She is now a regular columnist for several newspapers and magazines and organizes an annual culinary tour to her native Morocco. She is the author of several cookbooks, including her latest, *The Vegetarian Table: North Africa* (Chronicle Books).

- *Pasta with Blackened Fish & Caper Salsa (page 78)*

Cafe Pacifica This well-seasoned restaurant is located in the historic Old Town district of San Diego. It features Mediterranean seafood cuisine, with an emphasis on fresh fish, and boasts alfresco dining in an interior patio.

- *Seafood Fettuccine (page 72)*

Joseph Savino Joseph Savino is the executive chef of *Trattoria Acqua* in La Jolla, California. He received his formal training at Ecole de Cuisine La Varenne in Paris, receiving a Grand Diplome in cuisine in 1982. He is skilled in all aspects of Mediterranean cuisine, gaining most of his knowledge firsthand during trips to France, Italy, Greece, Spain and Morocco. In 1993 he was selected as one of the tops chefs in America by the Chefs of America Association.

- *Penne with Sicilian Tomato & Olive Sauce (page 34)*
- *Linguine with Mussels & Calamari (page 84)*

Helene Siegel Helene Siegel is a Los Angeles based cooking instructor and author of the best-selling *Totally Cookbook* series (including *Totally Garlic*) published by Celestial Arts.

- *Linguine Garlic Arrabiata (page 30)*

Edmund Osterland, MS Edmund Osterland is the wine editor of *Pasta Press* magazine. He has the distinguished honor of being the first American ever to pass the grueling Master Sommelier exam—recognized by many as the most difficult wine tasting exam in the world. He teaches wine education and appreciation courses and serves as a consultant to the industry. One of his special areas of expertise is on the affinity of food and wine, or how to pair wine with food for maximum flavor synergism.

- *All Wine Picks*

The 10 Commandments for Preparing Perfect Pasta

I. **Thou shalt not answer thy telephone while cooking pasta.**

You will jeopardize commandment #VII.

II. **Thou shalt cook thy pasta in a large pot.**

Your pasta will cook evenly and taste better if cooked in lots of water. Use at least 6 quarts of water (in an 8 quart pot) per pound of pasta.

III. **Thou shalt always start with cold water.**

Starting with cold water ensures that your pasta won't pick up any "off" tastes from your hot water heater.

IV. **Thou shalt cook thy pasta in rapidly boiling water.**

Your pasta will get mushy otherwise.

V. **Thou shalt salt thy pasta water.**

Pasta cooked in unsalted water tastes bland. Use 1–2 tablespoons salt per gallon of water.

VI. **Thou shalt frequently stir thy pasta while cooking.**

Your pasta will cook evenly and won't stick together if stirred at regular intervals.

VII.   Thou shalt not overcook thy pasta.

Overcooked pasta tastes mushy, lacks flavor and texture, and falls apart. Pasta should be cooked "al dente," or "to the tooth," meaning that it's tender but still firm.

VIII.   Thou shalt not time thy pasta.

Listed cooking times are approximate. There are too many variables that make timing virtually impossible to do accurately and consistently. Instead, frequently test your pasta for doneness by biting into a strand during the last minutes of cooking. When it's "al dente," drain immediately.

IX.   Thou shalt prepare thy sauce before cooking thy pasta.

Always make sure your sauce is ready (or will be ready) the moment your pasta is done. Adding it to the pasta immediately ensures that your pasta won't stick together in a hopeless clump. Once sauced, serve immediately!

X.   Thou shalt not rinse thy pasta after cooking.

The two exceptions are: 1) If the pasta is going to be used in a cold pasta salad, or 2) If you accidentally overcooked the pasta (probably as a result of not heeding commandment #I) and need to stop the cooking process in a hurry.

Pasta & Garlic...

with Vegetables!

Garlic & Basil "Raw" Sauce

Serves 4

Since there's no cooking involved, this raw sauce is extremely fast and easy to prepare. It works equally well served hot as a main course, or at room temperature for a picnic or a pasta salad. And, since it accentuates rather than masks flavors, it's especially great with just about any type of flavored pasta.

PASTA

linguine, fettuccine or pasta of your choice (¾ pound dried or 1 pound fresh)

SAUCE

2 Roma tomatoes, finely diced

½ teaspoon salt, or to taste

20–25 fresh basil leaves, chiffonade (see Tips on next page)

1½ tablespoons olive oil (divided use)

3–4 cloves garlic, minced

¼ cup freshly grated Parmesan

2 tablespoons roasted pine nuts (optional)

ADVANCE PREPARATION - 10 MINUTES

Prepare tomatoes and basil as specified. Place tomatoes in a bowl. Salt to taste. Add basil and toss. Drizzle over ½ tablespoon olive oil, toss gently again, cover and set aside. **Ingredients may be prepared <u>up to 8 hours in advance</u> if refrigerated.**

FINAL PREPARATION - 10 MINUTES

1. Cook pasta in plenty of rapidly boiling salted water until *al dente*. Drain and place in a large, shallow serving bowl. Drizzle on 1 tablespoon olive oil and toss to coat pasta.

WINE PICK
Sauvignon Blanc

2. Add garlic and toss to evenly distribute garlic. Add tomato mixture and toss again.

3. Serve immediately, sprinkling a little Parmesan and some pine nuts over each dish at the table. — OR — Allow to cool to room temperature and serve as a pasta salad or at a picnic.

Chris Gluck

TIPS, HINTS & SHORT-CUTS

To cut basil leaves into **chiffonade** *strips, stack the leaves on top of each other, roll into a tight "cigar," and slice into 1/16" wide strips with a sharp knife.*

NUTRITION DATA
(per serving)

*Calories: **401***
*Calories from Fat: **18.4%***
*Total Fat: **8.2 g***
*Saturated Fat: **1.9 g***
*Cholesterol: **4 mg***
*Sodium: **372 mg***
*Carbohydrates: **68 g***
*Dietary Fiber: **2.8 g***
*Protein: **14 g***

Three Variations on a Squash Stir-Fry

Serves 4

Here are three impromptu variations on a recipe that illustrate how easy it is to prepare delicious pasta dishes "on the fly." The first is a simple squash stir-fry; the second is the same recipe deglazed with wine or stock, while the third uses the smoky flavor of flamed tequila as a deglazing liquid. Try all three to see which you prefer; then experiment with ingredients of your choice to create your own masterpiece.

PASTA
linguine, fettuccine or pasta of your choice (¾ pound dried or 1 pound fresh)

SAUCE
1 tablespoon olive oil

8 cloves garlic, minced

1 cup yellow Italian squash, sliced into ¼" thick bite-sized pieces

1 cup zucchini, sliced into ¼" thick "half moons"

¼ cup freshly grated Parmesan

*¾ –1 cup dry white wine, or fat-free chicken stock, or vegetable stock **(for variation #2)***

*¾ –1 cup gold tequila **(for variation #3)***

ADVANCE PREPARATION - 10 MINUTES
Prepare vegetables as specified.
Ingredients may be prepared up to 8 hours in advance if refrigerated.

FINAL PREPARATION - 20 MINUTES
1. Pre-heat a large stir-fry pan or skillet over medium heat. Add garlic and sauté until golden. Increase heat to high and add squash and zucchini. Stir-fry 6–8 minutes, or until vegetables are lightly browned but not soggy.

WINE PICK
Sauvignon Blanc

28

2. Meanwhile, cook pasta in plenty of rapidly boiling salted water until *al dente*. Drain and add pasta, still slightly dripping, directly to the stir-fry pan. (See Tips.) Toss thoroughly and serve immediately straight from the pan. Sprinkle Parmesan over each serving at the table.

Variation #2

1. Proceed through step #1 above. Then add wine or stock and stir to deglaze the pan. Reduce heat and simmer 8–10 minutes, or until liquid reduces by half.

2. Meanwhile, cook pasta in plenty of rapidly boiling salted water until *al dente*. Drain thoroughly and add directly to the sauce. Cook 1 minute longer, tossing gently to thoroughly coat pasta. Serve immediately straight from the pan. Sprinkle Parmesan over each serving at the table.

Variation #3

1. Proceed as in variation #2 above except substitute tequila for the wine or stock. Flame tequila in a small saucepan (see Tips on page 83) before adding to the pan. Once the flame goes out, let tequila reduce by half and proceed as above.

Chris Gluck

Tips on page 83

TIPS, HINTS & SHORT-CUTS

*By adding cooked pasta that is still dripping with its cooking water directly to a stir-fry, the water droplets will **deglaze** the pan and create a flavorful coating for the pasta.*

NUTRITION DATA
(per serving)

Calories: **388**

Calories from Fat: **14.9%**

Total Fat: **6.4 g**

Saturated Fat: **1.6 g**

Cholesterol: **4 mg**

Sodium: **102 mg**

Carbohydrates: **68 g**

Dietary Fiber: **3.2 g**

Protein: **14 g**

Linguine Garlic Arrabiata

Serves 4–6

In Italy, a hot, spicy dish is often labeled "arrabiata," which translates "furious." You can easily adjust the "furiousness" of this quick tomato sauce from extra-mild to extra-hot simply by increasing or decreasing the amount of red pepper flakes.

PASTA

linguine or pasta of your choice
(1 pound dried or 1¼ pounds fresh)

SAUCE

1 tablespoon olive oil
½ yellow onion, chopped
8 cloves garlic, roughly chopped
¾ –1 teaspoon (to taste) red pepper flakes
1 can (28 oz.) diced or crushed tomatoes
¼ cup Kalamata (Greek) olives, pitted and roughly chopped
2 tablespoons capers
2 tablespoons Italian parsley, chopped
salt and pepper, to taste

ADVANCE PREPARATION - 10 MINUTES

Prepare vegetables and olives as specified. (Chop parsley at the last minute.) **Ingredients may be prepared up to 8 hours in advance** *if refrigerated.*

FINAL PREPARATION - 35 MINUTES

1. Heat olive oil in a large stir-fry pan or skillet over medium heat. Add onion and cook until soft.

WINE PICK
Riesling

2. Increase heat to medium-high and add garlic and pepper flakes. Cook just to release garlic's aroma, about 1 minute.

3. Pour in tomatoes, juice and all. Reduce heat to a simmer and cook, uncovered, stirring occasionally, until thickened, about 12–15 minutes.

4. Stir in remaining sauce ingredients and cook over low heat 5 minutes.

5. Meanwhile, cook pasta in plenty of rapidly boiling salted water until *al dente*. Drain and place in a large, shallow, pre-heated serving bowl. Pour over the hot sauce, toss thoroughly, and serve immediately.

Helene Siegel

TIPS, HINTS & SHORT-CUTS

This versatile, spicy sauce may also be used as a base for additional ingredients. You can slice left-over baked chicken into small chunks and add directly to the finished sauce, or you can cook bite-sized pieces of raw chicken breasts or whole shrimp directly in it.

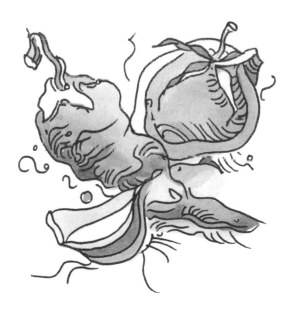

NUTRITION DATA
(per serving)

*Calories: **423***
*Calories from Fat: **13.7%***
*Total Fat: **6.5 g***
*Saturated Fat: **0.9 g***
*Cholesterol: **0 mg***
*Sodium: **234 mg***
*Carbohydrates: **78 g***
*Dietary Fiber: **5.4 g***
*Protein: **14 g***

Penne with Caramelized Shiitakes & Asparagus

Serves 6

This recipe uses an unusual technique whereby the various ingredients are basically "French fried" in smoking hot olive oil and then simmered in broth. At first glance, this appears to be an excessive amount of fat for the "under 20%" criteria; however, because the oil is so hot, it creates a crispy "skin" that stops the oil from being absorbed. This "skin" is also what seals in the juices and keeps everything tender. This process is called "caramelizing" and results is a luxurious dish with an incredibly complex blend of delicious flavors.

WINE PICK
Pinot Noir

PASTA
penne or thick pasta shape of your choice (1 pound dried or 1¼ pounds fresh)

SAUCE
½ cup olive oil (more or less)

½ pound shiitake mushroom caps, cut into ¼" thick slices

1 pound asparagus, sliced into 1" pieces

8 cloves garlic, thinly sliced (not minced)

1 quart fat-free chicken stock or roasted vegetable stock

1 tablespoon thyme, crushed

2 bunches baby spinach leaves (whole), or regular spinach leaves (torn in large pieces)

¾ cup freshly grated Parmesan

salt and pepper, to taste

ADVANCE PREPARATION - 15 MINUTES
Prepare vegetables as specified. Thoroughly clean spinach leaves.
Ingredients may be prepared up to 8 hours in advance if refrigerated. *(See step #3 for additional advance preparation notes.)*

Final Preparation - 60 minutes

1. Heat olive oil over high heat in a large stir-fry pan or kettle until it begins to smoke. Adjust quantity as necessary so it's about ½" deep. Immediately add mushrooms and sauté until caramelized. (See Tips) Remove with a slotted spoon and reserve on a paper towel.

2. Add asparagus and sauté until caramelized. Remove with a slotted spoon and reserve on a paper towel.

3. Add garlic slices and sauté until lightly browned but not burnt. Remove with a slotted spoon and reserve on a paper towel. (If making this dish for company, simplify final cooking by caramelizing mushrooms, asparagus and garlic several hours in advance. That way you can quickly throw everything together at the last minute.)

4. Carefully pour off and discard hot olive oil. While pan is still hot, immediately add back reserved mushrooms, asparagus and garlic. Immediately deglaze with a little stock. Add thyme and rest of stock, reduce heat, and simmer until stock reduces by half.

5. Meanwhile, cook pasta in plenty of rapidly boiling salted water until *al dente*. Drain and add directly to sauce pan. Add spinach and toss gently until it wilts into the pasta. Sprinkle on Parmesan and toss again. Adjust seasonings with salt and pepper if desired. Toss again and serve immediately straight from the pan.

Michael Chiarello

Tips, Hints & Short-Cuts

The secret to **caramelizing** *mushrooms and other ingredients without ending up with a soggy oily mess is to use extremely hot oil* <u>and</u> *to not crowd the ingredients as they cook. It will most likely be necessary to cook the mushrooms in 3–4 batches and the asparagus in 2–3 batches. Also, because adding the various ingredients to the oil will cause a temperature drop each time, make sure to allow a little time between batches to let the oil heat back up.*

Nutrition Data
(per serving)

Calories: **548**

Calories from Fat: **18.8%**

Total Fat: **11.7 g**

Saturated Fat: **3.2 g**

Cholesterol: **10 mg**

Sodium: **587 mg**

Carbohydrates: **92 g**

Dietary Fiber: **8.4 g**

Protein: **21 g**

33

Penne with Sicilian Tomato & Olive Sauce

Serves 4–6

This Sicilian-style dish convincingly demonstrates how easy it is to create delicious and healthy sauces without using fat. Rather than sautéing the ingredients in olive oil or butter, they are sweated in a fat-free liquid instead. Then by slowly reducing this liquid over low heat, the intense olive and orange flavors become even more concentrated—resulting in an extremely hearty, yet completely oil-free dish!

PASTA
penne, or pasta of your choice
(1 pound dried or 1¼ pound fresh)

SAUCE
6 cloves garlic, minced
2 yellow onions, thinly sliced lengthwise
1 cup dry white wine
4 cups chopped Roma tomatoes, or
1 (28 oz.) can diced tomatoes
1 cup Kalamata (Greek) olives, pitted and sliced
zest of 1 orange, grated
½ cup fresh basil, chiffonade
(see Tips on page 27)
black pepper, to taste

ADVANCE PREPARATION - 10 MINUTES
Prepare vegetables and olives as specified. (Slice basil and grate orange zest at the last minute.) **Ingredients may be prepared <u>up to 8 hours in advance</u> if refrigerated.**

FINAL PREPARATION - 40 MINUTES
1. Pre-heat a large skillet on high heat. Add garlic, onions and wine. Cover and reduce heat to a slow simmer. Sweat until

onions are meltingly soft, about 15–20 minutes.

2. Uncover and add tomatoes, olives, orange zest, and half the basil. Cook 10 minutes longer, or until sauce thickens slightly. Add salt to taste if desired.

3. Meanwhile, cook pasta in plenty of rapidly boiling salted water until *al dente*. Drain and transfer to a large shallow pre-heated serving bowl. Add sauce, remaining basil and black pepper. Toss thoroughly and serve immediately.

Joseph Savino

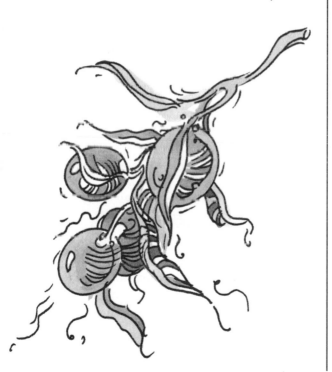

TIPS, HINTS & SHORT-CUTS

When grating orange zest, be extra careful to grate only the top thin orange layer. The white part directly underneath is very bitter and will ruin the flavor of this (or any) dish. Most kitchenware stores sell inexpensive citrus zesters designed to cut only through this thin layer. If one is not available, simply use the fine holes on a cheese grater instead.

NUTRITION DATA
(per serving)

*Calories: **488***
*Calories from Fat: **18.5%***
*Total Fat: **9.6 g***
*Saturated Fat: **1.2 g***
*Cholesterol: **0 mg***
*Sodium: **931 mg***
*Carbohydrates: **81 g***
*Dietary Fiber: **4.6 g***
*Protein: **14 g***

Pasta with Fresh Vegetables & Basil

Serves 6

PASTA

linguine, fettuccine or pasta of your choice (1 pound dried or 1¼ pounds fresh)

SAUCE

2 tablespoons olive oil

8 cloves garlic, minced

12 green onions, sliced into ½" pieces on the bias (both white and green parts)

1½ pounds asparagus (about 2 bunches), sliced into ½" pieces on the bias

1 pound assorted fresh mushrooms, sliced (your choice of varieties)

6 Roma tomatoes, cut into ¾" chunks

½ cup fresh basil, chiffonade (see Tips on page 27)

¼ cup Italian parsley, chopped

1½ –2 cups fat-free chicken stock or roasted vegetable stock

½ teaspoon freshly ground black pepper

½ cup freshly grated Parmesan

ADVANCE PREPARATION - 20 MINUTES

Prepare vegetables as specified. (Chop herbs at the last minute.) **Ingredients may be prepared up to 8 hours in advance if refrigerated.**

WINE PICK
Sauvignon Blanc

FINAL PREPARATION - 25 MINUTES

1. Heat olive oil in a large skillet or stir-fry pan over medium-high heat. Add garlic, green onions, asparagus and mushrooms. Stir-fry 6–8 minutes, or until asparagus is tender, but still firm.

2. Add tomatoes, basil and parsley. Toss well. Reduce heat to low and keep warm.

3. Meanwhile, cook pasta in plenty of rapidly boiling salted water until *al dente*. (See "runny" sauce Tips on page 49.)

4. Just before pasta is done, add stock and pepper to the vegetables. Bring to a simmer and immediately add cooked pasta directly to the same pan. Toss gently and allow to heat through on low for a few minutes.

5. Serve straight from the pan. Sprinkle a little Parmesan over each serving at the table.

Jeanne Jones

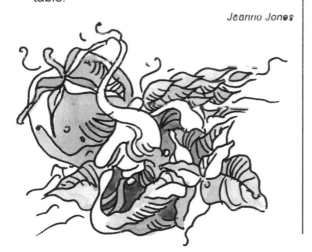

TIPS, HINTS & SHORT-CUTS

Be sure to take full advantage of seasonal produce by substituting or adding any readily available vegetables of your choice. Zucchinis, yellow squash, red or yellow bell peppers, artichoke hearts, broccoli florets and cauliflower florets all make wonderful additions and/or substitutions.

NUTRITION DATA
(per serving)

Calories: 537
Calories from Fat: 14.9%
Total Fat: 9.3 g
Saturated Fat: 2.3 g
Cholesterol: 6 mg
Sodium: 383 mg
Carbohydrates: 95 g
Dietary Fiber: 14.6 g
Protein: 24 g

37

Stir-Fried Ginger & Garlic Noodles

Serves 4 as an Appetizer

This versatile and tangy recipe is delicious served alone as an appetizer or side dish. Chilled, it also makes for an unusually tasty pasta salad. Or, with the addition of seafood, poultry, meat or tofu, it quickly transforms into a spicy Asian-style main course.

PASTA
angel hair or thin pasta of your choice (½ pound dried or fresh)

SAUCE
½ tablespoon canola oil

¼ – ½ cup ginger root, peeled and finely chopped

5 cloves garlic, finely chopped

2 tablespoons low-sodium soy sauce

2 tablespoons dry sherry or Chinese rice wine

1 teaspoon dark sesame oil

ADVANCE PREPARATION - 10 MINUTES
*Prepare ginger and garlic as specified. Combine soy sauce, wine and oil. **Ingredients may be prepared <u>up to 2 hours in advance</u> if refrigerated.***

FINAL PREPARATION - 15 MINUTES

1. Cook pasta in rapidly boiling water until *al dente*. Drain and reserve in a colander.

2. Heat canola oil in a wok or large stir-fry pan over medium-high heat. Add ginger and garlic and cook until they sizzle. Reduce heat to medium and stir-fry 1 minute longer.

WINE PICK
Riesling or Champagne

3. Add soy sauce, wine and sesame oil mixture. Mix well just to warm through. Immediately add reserved cooked pasta directly to the sauce. Toss gently until pasta re-heats and is completely coated. Serve immediately.

Jeanne Jones

If serving as a main course, quickly stir-fry bite-sized pieces of seafood, poultry, meat or firm tofu in canola oil prior to adding the ginger and garlic. Temporarily remove the cooked pieces with a slotted spoon and proceed with stir-frying the ginger and garlic. Then, just before adding the soy sauce, wine and sesame oil, add back the reserved cooked pieces and continue with the recipe.

NUTRITION DATA
(per serving)

*Calories: **258***
*Calories from Fat: **13.9%***
*Total Fat: **3.8 g***
*Saturated Fat: **0.4 g***
*Cholesterol: **0 mg***
*Sodium: **248 mg***
*Carbohydrates: **45 g***
*Dietary Fiber: **1.6 g***
*Protein: **8 g***

Wild Mushroom Pasta

The flavor secret in this recipe is to sauté thinly sliced fresh mushrooms until they lose nearly all their moisture. After they wilt and shrink in size, a rich tomato-herb broth then revives their intensely concentrated flavors.

Serves 4

PASTA
fusilli or spiral-shaped pasta of your choice (¾ pound dried or 1 pound fresh)

SAUCE
1 tablespoon olive oil

6 cloves garlic, minced

¼ cup shallots, minced

1¼ pounds assorted fresh mushrooms, cut into 1/8" thin slices (see Tips)

1¼ cups fat-free chicken stock

1½ tablespoons oyster sauce

1 tablespoon tomato paste

½ teaspoon sugar

¼ cup fresh basil leaves, chiffonade (see Tips on page 27)

1½ teaspoons fresh thyme, minced, or 1 teaspoon dried thyme, crushed

1 tablespoon cornstarch mixed with 1 tablespoon water

¾ cup freshly grated Parmesan

¾ cup Italian parsley, chopped

WINE PICK
Pinot Noir

ADVANCE PREPARATION - 20 MINUTES
Clean and prepare garlic, shallots, mushrooms and herbs as specified.

Combine chicken stock, oyster sauce,
tomato paste, sugar, basil and thyme.
Combine cornstarch and water.
Ingredients may be prepared <u>up to 4</u>
<u>hours in advance</u> if refrigerated.

FINAL PREPARATION - 30 MINUTES

1. Pre-heat a large stir-fry pan or skillet
over high heat. Add olive oil, garlic and
shallots. Sauté until garlic sizzles but does
not brown. Immediately add mushrooms
and stir-fry 2 minutes. Reduce heat to low
and continue cooking 10 minutes, or until
mushrooms wilt and lose nearly all their
moisture. Stir occasionally as necessary.

2. Meanwhile, cook pasta in plenty of
rapidly boiling salted water until *al dente.*
Drain and reserve.

3. After mushrooms wilt, add chicken
stock mixture. Bring to a simmer and add
reserved pasta directly to the pan. Toss
gently to mix. After pasta heats through,
add just enough cornstarch to the sauce so
it forms a thin glaze on the pasta. Stir in
Parmesan and mix thoroughly until
completely melted. Sprinkle on parsley,
toss lightly and serve immediately.

Hugh Carpenter

TIPS, HINTS & SHORT-CUTS

Use only firm-fleshed
mushrooms like cremini,
portobello or shiitake.
(Soft-textured mushrooms
like enoki or oyster are too
"mushy" for this recipe.)
While common button
mushrooms will also work
fine, by including a few of
the more exotic types, you
will transform this dish
from simple to sublime!

NUTRITION DATA
(per serving)

*Calories: **497***

*Calories from Fat: **18.3%***

*Total Fat: **10.1 g***

*Saturated Fat: **3.6 g***

*Cholesterol: **13 mg***

*Sodium: **849 mg***

*Carbohydrates: **79 g***

*Dietary Fiber: **4.5 g***

*Protein: **22 g***

41

Burnt Carrot Soup

Serves 4

I developed this recipe quite by accident with my daughter Erica. We'd been experimenting with using pureed roasted vegetables as a pasta sauce for her "Beyond Macaroni & Cheese" kids column in Pasta Press. We'd had more than our share of flops when we finally hit with this tasty flavor combination. Unfortunately the resulting puree was much too watery for a sauce. We were about to give up again when Erica came up with the idea of making soup with pasta instead of pasta with sauce. And that's exactly what we did!

WINE PICK
Sauvignon Blanc

PASTA

fusilli or spiral-shaped pasta of your choice (½ pound dried or fresh), or 1 pound gnocchi (see Tips)

SOUP

1 entire head of garlic, unpeeled

1 pound carrots, peeled

3 cups fat-free chicken stock or roasted vegetable stock

2 teaspoons dill

¼ teaspoon salt

1 teaspoon olive oil

¼ cup freshly grated Parmesan

ADVANCE PREPARATION - 60 MINUTES

*Roast and peel the garlic. (See Tips on page 57.) Roast the carrots on a grill or under a broiler until they almost begin to char in spots. **Ingredients may be prepared up to 8 hours in advance if refrigerated.** (See Tips for additional advance preparation notes.)*

FINAL PREPARATION - 25 MINUTES

1. Cut roasted carrots into ½" chunks and place into a saucepan. Add stock and

simmer, covered, for 10 minutes, or until carrots can be easily pierced with a fork.

2. While still hot, put cooked carrots and stock into a blender. Add dill, salt and reserved roasted garlic. Blend on high speed until completely pureed. Add olive oil and puree 30 seconds longer.

3. Meanwhile, cook pasta in plenty of rapidly boiling salted water until *al dente.* (If using gnocchi instead of pasta, cook them in boiling salted water just until they float to the surface.) Drain and place into individual serving bowls. Pour over the hot pureed carrot soup and sprinkle with a little Parmesan.

Erica Gluck

TIPS, HINTS & SHORT-CUTS

To eliminate almost all last minute preparation, the soup can be made completely in advance (except for cooking the pasta or gnocchi) and stored in the refrigerator up to several days. Then simply re-heat in the microwave when you're ready to serve. This recipe is also especially delicious with stir-fried gnocchi. (See instructions on page 45.)

NUTRITION DATA
(per serving)

Calories: **329**

Calories from Fat: **10.9%**

Total Fat: **3.8 g**

Saturated Fat: **1.3 g**

Cholesterol: **6 mg**

Sodium: **693 mg**

Carbohydrates: **58 g**

Dietary Fiber: **5.0 g**

Protein: **13 g**

Fried Gnocchi in Tomato Basil Cream Sauce

Serves 6

With words like "fried" and "cream" in the title, one could logically expect this recipe to be an exception to the "less than 20% of calories from fat" criteria. (It isn't. It comes in at under 19%.) Nevertheless, if you'd like to cut the fat even more, serve this dish with gnocchi that haven't been pan-fried (calories from fat drop to 14%), or with one pound of cooked pasta (calories from fat drop to 12%). Anyway you make it, it's sure to please!

WINE PICK
Chardonnay

PASTA

2 pounds gnocchi (Italian potato dumplings), or pasta of your choice (1 pound dried or 1¼ pounds fresh)

SAUCE

1 (28 oz.) can diced tomatoes

2 tablespoons olive oil (divided use)

½ teaspoon red pepper flakes

12 cloves garlic, minced (divided use)

3 tablespoons dry basil (divided use)

1 cup non-fat milk

1 tablespoon cornstarch blended with 1 tablespoon water

¼ cup freshly grated Parmesan

ADVANCE PREPARATION

(None)

FINAL PREPARATION - 40 MINUTES

1. Drain the juice from the canned tomatoes, reserving 1 cup.

2. Heat 1 tablespoon of the olive oil in a large saucepan over medium-high heat. Add pepper flakes and half of the garlic. Stir constantly until garlic is well browned but not burnt, about 30 seconds. Immediately add the drained tomatoes and

44

2 tablespoons of the basil. Reduce heat to medium-low and simmer until most of the rendered tomato liquids evaporate.

3. Meanwhile, combine 1 cup of reserved tomato juice with milk. Whisk in cornstarch and blend thoroughly until completely smooth. Heat gently in a saucepan or microwave to thicken.

4. Combine cooked tomatoes and tomato juice mixture in a blender. Puree until smooth. Return puree to a saucepan and simmer 10 minutes on lowest heat, stirring frequently.

5. Cook gnocchi in plenty of boiling salted water just until they float to the surface. Remove and reserve. (If using pasta instead of gnocchi, cook in plenty of rapidly boiling salted water until *al dente*. Skip step #6 and proceed directly to step #7, substituting cooked pasta for the gnocchi.)

6. Meanwhile, heat remaining tablespoon of olive oil in a large, non-stick stir-fry pan over medium heat. Add remaining garlic and sauté until golden. Increase heat to high and immediately add reserved gnocchi. Sprinkle in remaining basil. Cook until gnocchi are lightly browned on all sides, stirring gently but constantly with a wooden spoon to prevent sticking.

7. To serve, portion out gnocchi into 6 pre-warmed, large, shallow bowls. Spoon over sauce, sprinkle with Parmesan and serve.

Chris Gluck

TIPS, HINTS & SHORT-CUTS

Purists may turn up their noses at the admittedly unorthodox technique of __stir-frying gnocchi__, but personally it's my favorite way to prepare them. Not only does it add a delicious new crispy flavor dimension, but it also heats the gnocchi one step shy of scalding— ensuring that this is one dish that will always arrive to the table piping hot.

NUTRITION DATA
(per serving)

Calories: **334**

Calories from Fat: **18.7%**

Total Fat: **7.1 g**

Saturated Fat: **1.5 g**

Cholesterol: **3 mg**

Sodium: **637 mg**

Carbohydrates: **58 g**

Dietary Fiber: **4.0 g**

Protein: **11 g**

45

Pasta & Garlic...

Salsa Veracruz with Chicken & Pasta	48
Pasta with Roasted Chicken & Mushrooms	50
Easy Chili Pasta	52
Pasta with Grilled Eggplant & Chicken	54
Grilled Chicken with Roasted Tomato Cream	56

with Poultry!

Salsa Veracruz with Chicken & Pasta

Serves 4

Although traditionally served with red snapper, this classic Mexican sauce works equally well with chicken. The presence of lime juice, tomatoes, onions, chilies and cilantro are what one would expect to find in a Mexican dish. But what about the olive oil, olives and capers? These ingredients reflect the influence of Spain on indigenous ingredients. Interestingly enough, Spain also brought limes and cilantro to Mexico, but those products have become so integral to Mexican cooking that their origin has been forgotten.

PASTA

linguine, fettuccine or pasta of your choice (¾ pound dried or 1 pound fresh)

SAUCE

1/3 cup fresh squeezed lime juice
3 cups Roma tomatoes, diced
1 large red onion, diced
4 cloves garlic, minced
1–2 jalapeño peppers, seeded and finely diced
12 stuffed green olives, thinly sliced
2 tablespoons capers
4 teaspoons olive oil
¾ pound boneless, skinless chicken breasts, sliced into bite-sized pieces
2 tablespoons cilantro, minced
cilantro sprigs and lime wedges for garnish

ADVANCE PREPARATION - 25 MINUTES

*Squeeze lime juice. Prepare vegetables and chicken as specified. (Mince cilantro at the last minute.) **Ingredients may be prepared up to 8 hours in advance if refrigerated.***

WINE PICK
Sauvignon Blanc

48

Final Preparation - 30 minutes

1. Pour lime juice into a sauce pan. Add tomatoes, onion and garlic. Cover and simmer 8–10 minutes over medium heat.

2. Remove cover and add peppers, olives and capers. Simmer uncovered 3 minutes longer. Stir in olive oil.

3. Add chicken pieces and poach gently until done, approximately 7–10 minutes. Stir in cilantro once chicken is done.

4. Meanwhile, cook pasta in plenty of rapidly boiling salted water until *al dente.* (See Tips.) Drain and place into a large, shallow, pre-heated serving bowl. Ladle sauce over cooked pasta, garnish with cilantro sprigs and lime wedges, and serve immediately.

Arlyn Hackett

Tips, Hints & Short-Cuts

Whenever using a hot and runny sauce such as Salsa Veracruz, make sure to slightly undercook the pasta. The heat and wateriness of the sauce will continue to slowly cook the pasta for several more minutes. For a seafood entree, substitute red snapper pieces for the chicken. For a vegetarian entree simply eliminate the chicken.

Nutrition Data
(per serving)

*Calories: **506***
*Calories from Fat: **15.4%***
*Total Fat: **8.7 g***
*Saturated Fat: **1.3 g***
*Cholesterol: **40 mg***
*Sodium: **220 mg***
*Carbohydrates: **78 g***
*Dietary Fiber: **4.6 g***
*Protein: **29 g***

49

Pasta with Roasted Chicken & Mushrooms

Serves 4–6

This recipe originally specified duck breasts—a delicious option—but unfortunately one that's almost 40% of calories from fat. Fortunately, by lightly rubbing thick, skinless chicken breasts with a little olive oil, and then quickly roasting them on high heat, the result is similar to the delicious, "crispy" flavor typical of roast duck—at half the fat, and without any sacrifice to the taste buds!

WINE PICK
Pinot Noir

PASTA
fettuccine, linguine or pasta of your choice (¾ pound dried or 1 pound fresh)

SAUCE
2 large chicken breasts (about 1 pound total), skinned and boned

5 teaspoons olive oil (divided use)

1 pound assorted fresh mushrooms, sliced (See Tips)

6 cloves garlic, minced

1½ tablespoons thyme

2 cups fat-free chicken stock

1 cup dry white wine

1 cup very coarsely chopped fresh spinach or Swiss chard

ADVANCE PREPARATION - 20 MINUTES
*Skin and bone chicken breasts. Rub with 1 teaspoon olive oil. Season with salt and pepper if desired. Prepare vegetables as specified. **Ingredients may be prepared up to 8 hours in advance if refrigerated.***

FINAL PREPARATION - 45 MINUTES
1. Roast chicken breasts in a 425° oven until surface of chicken is golden and

50

crispy, but inside is still juicy and tender. Alternatively, grill chicken over high heat. (Either method will take approximately 12–15 minutes.) Set aside.

2. Meanwhile, heat 1 tablespoon olive oil in a large stir-fry pan or skillet over medium heat. Add mushrooms and sauté until they begin to sweat. Reduce heat slightly and continue cooking until all mushroom juices evaporate and mushrooms shrivel.

3. Add garlic and sauté until lightly browned.

4. Add thyme, stock and wine. Lower heat and simmer until liquids reduce by one third. Adjust seasoning with salt and pepper if desired.

5. While sauce reduces, heat 1 teaspoon olive oil in a small saucepan over medium heat. Add spinach or Swiss chard and cook just until wilted. Set aside.

6. Meanwhile, cook pasta in plenty of rapidly boiling salted water until *al dente*. Drain and divide half the pasta among 4 pre-heated, large, shallow bowls. Slice chicken breasts into bite-sized strips and place on top of pasta. Cover chicken with rest of pasta. Spoon mushroom broth over to almost cover pasta. Place wilted spinach or Swiss chard on top and serve immediately.

Mark Carter

TIPS, HINTS & SHORT-CUTS

Ideally use wild mushrooms for this dish. However, if they're not available (or are exorbitantly priced) regular button mushrooms will also work just fine— preferably with a handful of shiitake mushrooms thrown in for extra flavor.

NUTRITION DATA
(per serving)

Calories: **455**
Calories from Fat: **15.3%**
Total Fat: **7.1 g**
Saturated Fat: **1.1 g**
Cholesterol: **43 mg**
Sodium: **384 mg**
Carbohydrates: **59 g**
Dietary Fiber: **3.8 g**
Protein: **29 g**

Easy Chili Pasta

Serves a Crowd! (16–20)

Here's a simple but very tasty recipe that uses pasta shells, ground turkey and lots of vegetables in place of the higher-fat beef or pork found in most chili recipes.

PASTA
conchiglie or pasta shape of your choice
(1 pound dried)

SAUCE
1 yellow onion, chopped
1 red bell pepper, chopped
8 cloves garlic, minced
1½ pounds ground lean turkey (See Tips)
3 zucchinis, cut into ½" thick slices
1 pound mushrooms, quartered
½ cup chili powder
2 tablespoons Tabasco® sauce, or to taste
1 bag (16 oz.) frozen corn, rinsed
2 cans (15 oz. each) black beans,
   thoroughly rinsed and drained
2 cans (28 oz. each) diced tomatoes
2 cups tomato juice

ADVANCE PREPARATION - 15 MINUTES
Prepare vegetables as specified.
Ingredients may be prepared <u>up to 8 hours in advance</u> if refrigerated.

FINAL PREPARATION - 90 MINUTES
1. Put onion, bell pepper, garlic and turkey in a large kettle. Cook on medium heat 15 minutes, stirring occasionally.

WINE PICK
Riesling

2. Add zucchinis and mushrooms. Cook 10 minutes longer, stirring occasionally.

3. Reduce heat to low and add all remaining ingredients except pasta. When chili comes to a simmer, cook 30 minutes longer, stirring occasionally.

4. Meanwhile, cook pasta in plenty of rapidly boiling salted water until *al dente*. Drain and immediately rinse in cold water until pasta is completely cool.

5. When chili is done, add the drained, cooled pasta directly to the chili pot. Stir gently and simmer 2 minutes longer. Turn off heat and adjust seasoning with a little salt and/or hot sauce if desired. Serve in soup bowls.

Erica Gluck

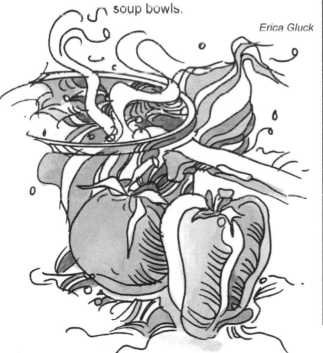

TIPS, HINTS & SHORT-CUTS

This recipe makes about 16–20 servings. You can cut back on the ingredient quantities if you want to make less, but I usually make the full recipe just so there will be leftovers. Like most chilis, it tastes even better the next day and it easily re-heats in a microwave. For a vegetarian option you can substitute baked eggplant chunks and more mushrooms for the turkey. You can also substitute kidney or pinto beans for the black beans.

NUTRITION DATA
(per serving)

*Calories: **313***
*Calories from Fat: **13.8%***
*Total Fat: **5.0 g***
*Saturated Fat: **1.0 g***
*Cholesterol: **26 mg***
*Sodium: **380 mg***
*Carbohydrates: **51 g***
*Dietary Fiber: **9.3 g***
*Protein: **21 g***

Pasta with Grilled Eggplant & Chicken

Serves 6

Grills aren't just for meat! This recipe, and the one that follows, give your grill a workout—not only with chicken, but also with eggplant, peppers, onions, garlic and even whole tomatoes! And since both recipes share many of the same ingredients, they're easy to prepare together. Why not make both for your next backyard barbecue?

PASTA
plain or spinach fettuccine or linguine (1 pound dried or 1¼ pounds fresh)

SAUCE
1 large eggplant, peeled and cut into ¾" thick slices

kosher salt

3 boneless, skinless chicken breasts (about 1¼ pounds total)

2½ tablespoons olive oil

1½ ounces (about ½ cup) sun-dried tomatoes, cut into thin strips

2 bell peppers (1 green, 1 red), roasted, peeled, seeded and sliced into thin strips

½ cup dry white wine

1 whole head garlic, roasted and peeled

2–4 teaspoons pureed chipotles en adobo (See Glossary)

1½ cups fat-free chicken stock

¼ cup freshly grated Parmesan

ADVANCE PREPARATION - 60 MINUTES
Squeeze out the eggplant's bitterness with kosher salt. (See Tips) Roast bell peppers and slice as specified, taking care to reserve any juices. (See "Roasting Peppers" in Glossary) Roast and peel

WINE PICK
Chardonnay

garlic. (See Tips on page 57.) **Ingredients**
may be prepared _up to 8 hours in_
advance if refrigerated.

FINAL PREPARATION - 40 MINUTES

1. Grill or broil chicken breasts 3–5
minutes per side, or until still very "rare."
Slice into thin, bite-sized strips. Reserve.

2. Heat olive oil over medium-high heat in
a large stir-fry pan or skillet. Cut eggplant
slices into ¾" cubes and sauté for 7–8
minutes. While eggplant cooks, rehydrate
sun-dried tomatoes in ½ cup warm water
for 5 minutes.

3. Drain sun-dried tomatoes and add to
eggplant. Immediately add grilled peppers
with their juices. Sauté together 2 minutes
longer. Deglaze with wine.

4. Add roasted garlic (mash it first if it's
not already like a paste), chipotles to taste
and chicken stock. Simmer on low until
sauce thickens to your liking, about 5–10
minutes. Add reserved chicken slices and
simmer several minutes to heat through
and to allow flavors to blend. Season to
taste with salt and pepper if desired.

5. Meanwhile, cook pasta in plenty of
rapidly boiling salted water until *al dente*.
Drain and place in a large pre-heated
serving bowl. Add sauce and toss gently to
mix. Sprinkle on Parmesan and serve
immediately.

Ingrid Croce

TIPS, HINTS & SHORT-CUTS

*To **eliminate the**
bitterness in eggplant,
first sprinkle the eggplant
slices with kosher salt.
Next layer the slices in a
colander (in the sink).
Place a clean, heavy
object on top to weigh
them down. (I use a large
pot filled with water.)
Leave on for 30 minutes.
After 30 minutes, blot the
slices dry with a paper
towel and proceed with the
recipe.*

NUTRITION DATA
(per serving)

*Calories: **499***
*Calories from Fat: **16.9%***
*Total Fat: **9.0 g***
*Saturated Fat: **1.8 g***
*Cholesterol: **47 mg***
*Sodium: **266 mg***
*Carbohydrates: **68 g***
*Dietary Fiber: **5.3 g***
*Protein: **31 g***

Grilled Chicken with Roasted Tomato Cream

Serves 6

Like the preceding recipe, this dish takes advantage of grilling not only chicken, but vegetables as well. The wonderful roasted smokiness that results permeates the entire dish with complex waves of delicious flavors.

PASTA

farfalle (bow ties) or pasta of your choice (1 pound dried or 1¼ pounds fresh)

SAUCE

2 tablespoons olive oil (divided use)

1 teaspoon liquid smoke (optional)

3 boneless, skinless chicken breasts (about 1¼ pounds total)

1–2 teaspoons cayenne

1 whole head garlic, roasted and peeled

2 pounds Roma tomatoes, stems removed

2 yellow onions, peeled and quartered

2 cups fat-free chicken stock

2–4 teaspoons pureed chipotles en adobo (See Glossary)

2 tablespoons red chile powder

2 teaspoons marjoram

1½ teaspoons salt

½ cup light cream (half & half)

½ cup cilantro, chopped

ADVANCE PREPARATION - 60 MINUTES

Combine 1 tablespoon olive oil with liquid smoke. Brush mixture on chicken breasts and season with cayenne to taste. Place in a plastic zipper lock freezer bag to marinate for at least 30 minutes. Roast and peel garlic. (See Tips) Prepare

WINE PICK
Pinot Noir

vegetables as specified. **Ingredients may be prepared up to 8 hours in advance if refrigerated.** *(See step #3 for additional advance preparation notes.)*

FINAL PREPARATION - 60 MINUTES

1. Grill or broil whole tomatoes until skins blister and burn in spots. Grill onions until soft and slightly burned in spots.

2. Put roasted garlic, tomatoes, onions, chicken stock, chipotles to taste, chile powder, marjoram, salt and 1 tablespoon olive oil in a blender. Puree until smooth. (Depending on blender capacity, this may need to be done in 2 stages. You should end up with about 5 cups of liquid.)

3. Pour tomato puree into a large kettle and simmer uncovered until sauce reduces to 4 cups, about 20 minutes. (To facilitate quicker final preparation, everything up to this point may be done up to 2 days in advance if kept refrigerated.) Stir in cream and keep warm on lowest possible heat.

4. Grill or broil chicken 3–5 minutes per side, or until still "rare." Slice into thin, bite-sized strips and add to sauce. Keep warm on lowest heat several minutes longer to heat through and to allow flavors to blend.

5. Meanwhile, cook pasta in plenty of rapidly boiling salted water until al dente. Drain and place in a large pre-heated serving bowl. Add sauce and toss gently to mix. Sprinkle on cilantro and serve.

Chris Gluck

TIPS, HINTS & SHORT-CUTS

*To **roast garlic**, place an entire unpeeled head on a pie tin and bake in a 400° oven until the skin turns brown and the cloves are soft and paste-like, about 40–50 minutes. When cool enough to handle, squeeze the cloves out of their skins. They should be soft enough to squeeze out like toothpaste. If not, simply peel conventionally and mash into a paste.*

NUTRITION DATA
(per serving)

*Calories: **498***

*Calories from Fat: **16.4%***

*Total Fat: **9.0 g***

*Saturated Fat: **2.4 g***

*Cholesterol: **52 mg***

*Sodium: **829 mg***

*Carbohydrates: **72 g***

*Dietary Fiber: **5.3 g***

*Protein: **31 g***

Penne with Smoked Chicken Sausage

Serves 4

Sausages are turning up in an increasing variety of exotic flavors, many of which utilize fillings that are much lower in fat than typical pork sausage. This recipe utilizes one of our favorites—smoked chicken. By allowing the sausage to gently simmer in a reducing chicken broth, its wonderful smoky flavor permeates the entire dish.

PASTA

penne or thick pasta shape of your choice (¾ pound dried or 1 pound fresh)

SAUCE

2 teaspoons olive oil

4 cloves garlic, minced

2 cups bell peppers (your choice of colors), sliced into ¼" strips

1 cup zucchini, julienne

1 cup carrots, julienne

½ cup mushrooms (preferably shiitakes), sliced

½ pound smoked chicken sausage, grilled, broiled or sautéed, and sliced into ½" pieces (See Tips)

1½ cups fat-free chicken stock

1 teaspoon thyme

1 teaspoon rosemary

¼ cup freshly grated Parmesan

ADVANCE PREPARATION - 30 MINUTES

Prepare vegetables as specified. Cook sausage and slice as specified.
Ingredients may be prepared <u>up to 8 hours in advance</u> if refrigerated.

WINE PICK
Merlot

Final Preparation - 30 minutes

1. Heat olive oil in a large non-stick stir-fry pan or skillet over medium-high heat. Add garlic and sauté 1 minute. Add bell peppers and sauté 3–5 minutes, or until soft.

2. Add zucchini, carrots, mushrooms and sausage. Stir-fry 3 minutes. Reduce heat to medium and add chicken stock, thyme and rosemary. Simmer gently until stock reduces by half.

3. Meanwhile, cook pasta in plenty of rapidly boiling salted water until *al dente*. Drain and reserve.

4. Add cooked pasta directly to sauce, toss gently, and allow to heat through. Sprinkle on Parmesan, toss again, and serve immediately straight from the pan.

Daniel McKenna

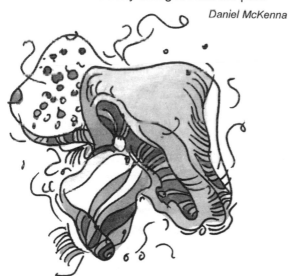

Tips, Hints & Short-Cuts

Smoked chicken sausage is available in most well-stocked supermarkets and delis. There are many varieties, including some with apple bits and Chardonnay, that are especially tasty. Most contain fully cooked chicken meat and need only to be browned for a few minutes on a hot grill or under a broiler.

Nutrition Data

(per serving)

Calories: **515**
Calories from Fat: **18.8%**
Total Fat: **10.8 g**
Saturated Fat: **3.0 g**
Cholesterol: **47 mg**
Sodium: **603 mg**
Carbohydrates: **82 g**
Dietary Fiber: **6.8 g**
Protein: **23 g**

59

Pasta Marrakech with Chicken

Serves 4

Flavor combinations typical of Morocco—namely honey, lemon, paprika, crushed red pepper, cilantro, mint and leathery black olives—magically blend to create this refreshing and exceptionally delicious recipe.

PASTA
fusilli or spiral shaped pasta of your choice (¾ pound dried or 1 pound fresh)

SAUCE
8 cloves garlic, minced

3 tablespoons ginger root, peeled and grated

½ cup fresh cilantro, chopped

½ cup fresh mint leaves, chopped

½ cup fat-free chicken stock

½ cup freshly squeezed lemon juice

6 tablespoons honey

1 tablespoon ground cumin

1 tablespoon sweet paprika

1 tablespoon cornstarch

½–1 teaspoon red pepper flakes

1 pound skinless, boneless chicken breasts, cut into thin bite-sized pieces

1 tablespoon olive oil

½ cup oil-cured black olives (or Kalamata olives), pitted and coarsely chopped

ground nutmeg, to taste

ADVANCE PREPARATION - 30 MINUTES
Prepare a sauce by combining garlic, ginger, cilantro, mint, chicken stock, lemon juice, honey, cumin, paprika, cornstarch

WINE PICK
Pinot Noir

and pepper flakes. *Mix thoroughly and set aside. Cut chicken into bite-sized pieces and place into a plastic zipper lock freezer bag. Add 3 tablespoons of the sauce mixture, seal, shake well and allow chicken to marinate at least ½ hour or up to 8 hours in the refrigerator. Pit and chop olives.* **Ingredients may be prepared <u>up to 8 hours in advance</u> if refrigerated.**

FINAL PREPARATION - 15 MINUTES

1. Cook pasta in plenty of rapidly boiling salted water until *al dente*. Drain and reserve.

2. While pasta cooks, pre-heat a large stir-fry pan or skillet over high heat. Add olive oil. When oil gives off a wisp of smoke, add chicken and stir-fry until it loses its raw outside color.

3. Add reserved sauce, olives and cooked pasta directly to the pan. Reduce heat to medium and stir and toss gently until everything is evenly combined and heated through. Serve immediately straight from the pan. Dust a little nutmeg over each serving at the table.

Hugh Carpenter

TIPS, HINTS & SHORT-CUTS

If you have left-over baked chicken, you can skip step #2. Simply cut the already cooked chicken into bite-sized pieces and add along with the olive oil directly to the warmed sauce in step #3. For a vegetarian entree, omit the chicken altogether and substitute vegetable stock for the chicken stock.

NUTRITION DATA
(per serving)

Calories: **638**

Calories from Fat: **16.1%**

Total Fat: **11.5 g**

Saturated Fat: **1.7 g**

Cholesterol: **53 mg**

Sodium: **632 mg**

Carbohydrates: **101 g**

Dietary Fiber: **3.3 g**

Protein: **34 g**

Gnocchi with Italian "Sausage" & Tomatoes

Serves 4

This sauce is typical of a traditional sausage and tomato sauce—without the sausage! Usually made by removing the casings from Italian sausages, and then crumbling and cooking the sausage meat, this sauce differs in that it allows you to control the ingredients of the "sausage." (After all, sausage, is nothing more than ground meat blended with various seasonings and fillers.) By processing your own chicken meat with a few herbs, you can easily replicate the flavor of Italian sausage—without all the fat!

WINE PICK
Chianti

PASTA
1 pound gnocchi (Italian potato dumplings), or pasta of your choice (¾ pound dried or 1 pound fresh)

SAUCE
1 tablespoon olive oil

1 yellow onion, chopped

¾ pound boneless, skinless chicken breast pieces

2 tablespoons basil

1 tablespoon granulated garlic

2 teaspoons fennel seed

1 teaspoon red pepper flakes

1 (28 oz.) can diced tomatoes

½ teaspoon salt

2 tablespoons tomato paste

ADVANCE PREPARATION - 15 MINUTES
*Chop onion. Process chicken, basil, granulated garlic, fennel seed and pepper flakes in a food processor fitted with a steel blade until chicken is thoroughly blended with the seasonings. **Ingredients may be prepared <u>up to 8 hours in advance</u> if refrigerated.** (See step #3 for additional advance preparation notes.)*

Final Preparation - 45 minutes

1. Heat olive oil in a saucepan over medium-low heat. Add onions and cook, stirring occasionally, until onions are golden brown but still limp.

2. Add ground chicken mixture to browned onions. Increase heat to medium and cook for 7–8 minutes, stirring frequently to break the ground chicken into small chunks.

3. Add tomatoes (juice and all), salt and tomato paste. Reduce heat to low and simmer for at least 20 minutes, stirring occasionally. (Time permitting, make this sauce several hours in advance to allow the flavors to develop even more.)

4. Cook gnocchi in boiling salted water until they float. (If using pasta instead of gnocchi, cook in plenty of rapidly boiling water until *al dente*.) Drain and place in a large serving bowl. Pour over the sauce, toss thoroughly and serve immediately.

Chris Gluck

Tips, Hints & Short-Cuts

The amount of sauce in this recipe is very liberal. If you prefer a less "soupy" finished product, add more gnocchi, scale back the sauce ingredients, or save the extra sauce for another use. This sauce is also chunky and somewhat "loose." If you prefer a thicker sauce, double the amount of tomato paste, break the ground chicken into ¼" chunks (with a stiff wire whisk), and increase the simmering time until the sauce thickens more.

Nutrition Data
(per serving)

*Calories: **341***
*Calories from Fat: **15.2%***
*Total Fat: **5.9 g***
*Saturated Fat: **0.9 g***
*Cholesterol: **40 mg***
*Sodium: **597 mg***
*Carbohydrates: **50 g***
*Dietary Fiber: **6.4 g***
*Protein: **24 g***

Caribbean Pasta with Chicken

Serves 4

Caribbean cooking is a fusion of rich cooking traditions from around the world. This recipe uses one of our favorite sauces in which the flavors of tomato, curry, allspice, chilis and ginger play starring roles.

PASTA
fusilli, radiatore or other spiral shaped pasta (½ pound dried or fresh)

SAUCE
1 red bell pepper, finely diced
1½ cups tomatoes (fresh or canned), peeled, seeded and chopped
1½ teaspoons curry powder
½ teaspoon ground allspice
½ cup fat-free chicken stock
¼ cup Grand Marnier or orange juice
2 tablespoons soy sauce
1 tablespoon brown sugar
2 teaspoons cornstarch
½ –1 teaspoon Chinese chili paste
1½ tablespoons canola oil
4 cloves garlic, minced
1 tablespoon ginger root, peeled and grated
½ cup green onions (both white and green parts), thinly sliced
½ pound boneless, skinless chicken breast, sliced into thin bite-sized strips
½ cup cilantro, chopped

ADVANCE PREPARATION - 30 MINUTES
Prepare a sauce by combining bell pepper, tomatoes, curry, allspice, chicken stock, Grand Marnier (or orange juice), soy

WINE PICK
Gewurztraminer

64

sauce, brown sugar, cornstarch, and chili paste. Mix thoroughly and set aside. Prepare garlic, ginger, and green onions as specified. Slice chicken into strips. (Chop cilantro at the last minute.) **Ingredients may be prepared up to 8 hours in advance if refrigerated.**

FINAL PREPARATION - 20 MINUTES

1. Cook pasta in plenty of rapidly boiling salted water until *al dente*. Drain and reserve.

2. While pasta is cooking, pre-heat a large stir-fry pan or skillet over high heat. Add canola oil, garlic and ginger. Sauté until garlic begins to sizzle, about 30 seconds.

3. Add green onions and stir-fry 30 seconds.

4. Immediately stir in reserved sauce, bring to a rapid boil, reduce heat to medium, and cook until it begins to thicken, about 2–3 minutes.

5. Add chicken pieces and cook in the sauce until almost done, about 4–5 minutes.

6. Reduce heat to low and stir in reserved pasta. Stir gently until everything is evenly combined and chicken is completely cooked. Taste and adjust seasonings, especially for salt. Sprinkle on cilantro, toss lightly and serve straight from the pan.

Hugh Carpenter

TIPS, HINTS & SHORT-CUTS

For variety substitute a blend of chopped mint and basil for the cilantro, or omit the chili paste and add finely minced fresh serrano or scotch bonnet chilis. You can also substitute raw shrimp (shell, devein, and split lengthwise first) for the chicken.

NUTRITION DATA
(per serving)

*Calories: **469***
*Calories from Fat: **16.0%***
*Total Fat: **7.7 g***
*Saturated Fat: **0.8 g***
*Cholesterol: **53 mg***
*Sodium: **562 mg***
*Carbohydrates: **60 g***
*Dietary Fiber: **3.5 g***
*Protein: **31 g***

65

Pasta & Garlic...

with Seafood!

Pasta with Seared Scallops

Serves 4–6

Traditionally smothered in a rich sauce containing lots of cream and butter, the typical pasta and scallops recipe is similar to Fettuccine Alfredo fatwise. In this recipe, however, two separate techniques (deglazing and reduction—see Tips) are used together to create an intensely flavored sauce without the addition of fat!

PASTA
linguine, fettuccine or pasta of your choice (1 pound dried or 1¼ pounds fresh)

SAUCE
1 tablespoon olive oil
1 pound fresh bay scallops
juice from 1 lemon
8 cloves garlic, minced
1 cup dry white wine
½ cup Italian parsley, chopped

ADVANCE PREPARATION - 5 MINUTES
Peel and mince garlic. Chop parsley.
Ingredients may be prepared <u>up to 8 hours in advance</u> if refrigerated.

FINAL PREPARATION - 20 MINUTES

1. Heat olive oil in a large non-stick stir-fry pan or skillet over high heat. Add scallops and stir-fry 1½ minutes, deglazing with lemon juice as necessary.

2. Immediately remove scallops with a slotted spoon, leaving olive oil and juices behind. Reserve.

3. Reduce heat and add garlic. Simmer on low, allowing lemon and scallop "juices" to slowly evaporate. When garlic turns

WINE PICK
Chardonnay

golden, increase heat slightly and deglaze the pan with a splash of wine. Then add balance of wine and simmer slowly until reduced by half.

4. Add back reserved scallops and parsley. Gently heat through, taking care not to overcook scallops.

5. Meanwhile, cook pasta in plenty of rapidly boiling water until *al dente*. Drain and add directly to the sauce. Toss thoroughly and heat through for 1 minute. Serve immediately straight from the pan.

Chris Gluck

Spicy Singapore Prawns

Serves 4

PASTA

1 package (6 ounces) bean thread noodles (See Tips)

SAUCE

1¼ cups rice vinegar (divided use)

1 cup sugar

1 cup water

1 tablespoon canola oil

1 pound large raw shrimp, peeled and deveined

2 tablespoons garlic, minced

2 tablespoons green onions, chopped

1 tablespoon fresh cilantro, minced

2–3 teaspoons red pepper flakes

¼ cup dry white wine or water

1 tablespoon soy sauce

ADVANCE PREPARATION - 20 MINUTES

Combine 1 cup of the vinegar with sugar and water. Stir thoroughly until sugar completely dissolves. Peel and devein shrimp. Prepare garlic and green onions as specified. (Mince cilantro at the last minute.) **Ingredients may be prepared *up to 8 hours in advance* if refrigerated.**

WINE PICK
Riesling

70

Final Preparation - 15 minutes

1. Cook bean thread noodles in a large pot of boiling water until tender, about 5 minutes. While noodles cook, heat sugar/vinegar mixture in a large bowl in a microwave until quite warm but not burning hot. Drain cooked noodles and add to the sugar/vinegar mixture, tossing to coat the noodles. Set aside to marinate, keeping warm.

2. Heat canola oil in a large stir-fry pan or skillet over high heat. Add shrimp and cook 1 minute. Stir in garlic, green onions, cilantro and pepper flakes. Add wine (or water), remaining ¼ cup rice vinegar and soy sauce. Bring just to a boil and then turn off the heat. Adjust seasonings if necessary, adding more soy sauce or pepper flakes if desired.

3. Thoroughly drain the warm noodles, discarding marinade. Divide noodles among 4 pre-warmed shallow bowls. Arrange shrimp on top of noodles, spoon over sauce and serve immediately

Scott Fraser

Tips, Hints & Short-Cuts

__Bean thread noodles__ are a semi-transparent type of Asian pasta made from mung bean starch. They are readily available in most supermarkets. In the stores they will look like bundles of stiff nylon fishing line packaged in a plastic bag. However, once cooked, they turn almost clear; hence they are sometimes called "glass noodles." To prepare for recipe use, soak them in hot tap water for 30 minutes, or boil gently for 3–5 minutes.

Nutrition Data

(per serving)

*Calories: **354***

*Calories from Fat: **14.1%***

*Total Fat: **5.4 g***

*Saturated Fat: **0.6 g***

*Cholesterol: **173 mg***

*Sodium: **383 mg***

*Carbohydrates: **50 g***

*Dietary Fiber: **1.2 g***

*Protein: **24 g***

71

Seafood Fettuccine

Serves 4–6

Feel free to use other types of seafood in this spicy recipe. Crab claws, lobster tails, mussels, clams, scallops and calamari all make great substitutions or additions. And be sure to serve with plenty of hot, crusty French bread for dipping into the brothy sauce!

PASTA

fettuccine, linguine or pasta of your choice (¾ pound dried or 1 pound fresh)

SAUCE

1½ tablespoons olive oil

2 tablespoons garlic, minced

2 red bell peppers, sliced into ¼" strips

1 pound cod (or other white fish) fillets, cut into 1" pieces

¾ pound raw shrimp, peeled and deveined

3 cups tomatoes, diced

1–2 tablespoons spicy seasoning (use your favorite store-bought brand or make your own with the recipe in Tips)

2 cups fish stock (or mix ¾ cup bottled clam juice with 1¼ cups fat-free chicken stock)

½ cup green onions, chopped

2 teaspoons cornstarch mixed with 2 teaspoons cold water

ADVANCE PREPARATION - 25 MINUTES

Prepare vegetables and seafood as specified. **Ingredients may be prepared up to 8 hours in advance *if refrigerated*.**

WINE PICK
Viognier

72

Final Preparation - 20 minutes

1. Heat olive oil in a large stir-fry pan or skillet over high heat. Add garlic and sauté 30 seconds. Add bell peppers and stir-fry 1 minute. Add fish and shrimp and stir-fry 2 minutes longer.

2. Add tomatoes and seasoning to taste. Stir constantly until tomato juices evaporate, about 1 minute. Deglaze pan with a splash of stock; then add balance of stock and green onions. Reduce heat when sauce begins to simmer. Add cornstarch mixture and simmer gently, stirring frequently, until sauce thickens

3. Meanwhile, cook pasta in plenty of rapidly boiling salted water until *al dente*. Drain and add directly to the sauce. Toss gently and serve immediately straight from the pan.

Cafe Pacifica

Tips, Hints & Short-Cuts

To make your own **spicy seasoning mix,** *combine:*

1 T. salt
1 T. onion powder
1 T. paprika
1 T. dried thyme
½ T. white pepper
½ T. cayenne
½ T. ground black pepper
½ T. red chile powder

Put all ingredients in a glass jar and shake for 1 minute to mix thoroughly. Store in an airtight container away from heat and light. Yields 6 tablespoons.

Nutrition Data
(per serving)

Calories: **545**
Calories from Fat: **14.1%**
Total Fat: **8.1 g**
Saturated Fat: **1.2 g**
Cholesterol: **142 mg**
Sodium: **519 mg**
Carbohydrates: **70 g**
Dietary Fiber: **4.7 g**
Protein: **41 g**

Pasta with Mussels & Garlic in White Wine

Serves 4–6

We had our very first encounter with mussels during a visit to San Francisco in the early '80's. Discovering a small restaurant advertising buckets of fresh steamed mussels as the evening's special, we decided to take a chance. They were incredible! So incredible that we went back for the next three evenings! Returning home, we quickly learned how easy mussels were to cook and began experimenting with lower fat versions of the dish we so enjoyed in San Francisco. Here's one of our favorites.

PASTA

penne, conchiglie or any thick pasta (¾ pound dried or 1 pound fresh)

SAUCE

1 tablespoon olive oil

10 cloves garlic, minced

2 leeks, cleaned and thinly sliced

1 yellow onion, chopped

1 red or yellow bell pepper, diced

½ bottle dry white wine (more or less)

1 cup water

4 tomatoes, peeled and coarsely chopped

1 bunch Italian parsley, loosely chopped

2 pounds mussels, well scrubbed (see Tips)

ADVANCE PREPARATION - 40 MINUTES

*Clean and prepare vegetables as specified. Scrub and de-beard mussels. (Store mussels in a large bowl covered with a wet cloth in the refrigerator if they won't be cooked right away. **Ingredients may be prepared <u>up to 8 hours in advance</u> if refrigerated.***

FINAL PREPARATION - 45 MINUTES

1. Heat olive oil in a large heavy kettle on medium-low heat. Add garlic and sauté

WINE PICK
Sauvignon Blanc

74

until golden. Increase heat to medium and add leeks, onions and peppers. Cook until leeks are browned but still limp.

2. Deglaze kettle with a small amount of wine. After any burned bits are dissolved, add the rest of the wine and the water. Increase heat to medium-high and bring to a steady simmer. Add tomatoes and parsley and cook a few minutes longer.

3. Add mussels and cover kettle with a tight fitting lid. Cook until mussels open; then simmer 2–3 minutes longer before turning off heat. Leave covered.

4. Meanwhile, cook pasta in plenty of rapidly boiling water until *al dente*. (See "runny" sauce Tips on page 49.) Drain and put into a large, shallow serving bowl. Arrange cooked mussels (shell and all) and cooked vegetables on top of the pasta. Pour 1 cup of broth over the top and serve immediately.

5. Pour remaining broth into individual bowls or mugs and serve with plenty of crusty bread for dipping.

Chris Gluck

TIPS, HINTS & SHORT-CUTS

*To **clean mussels**, scrub them with a scouring pad under cold running water to remove barnacles and deposits. Use pliers to remove the especially stubborn "beard" if necessary. After cooking, make sure to discard any that don't open. Any left-over cooked mussels may be stored in extra broth and used as a base for mussel bisque or chowder. (We frequently cook extras just so we'll have leftovers for this purpose.)*

NUTRITION DATA
(per serving)

Calories: **571**
Calories from Fat: **15.0%**
Total Fat: **8.5 g**
Saturated Fat: **1.4 g**
Cholesterol: **51 mg**
Sodium: **553 mg**
Carbohydrates: **75 g**
Dietary Fiber: **4.6 g**
Protein: **33 g**

Chinese Pasta with Bay Scallops

Serves 4

If scallops aren't available, this refreshingly tangy and versatile dish can also be made with shrimp or even bite-sized pieces of firm white fish.

PASTA

angel hair or thin pasta of your choice (¾ pound dried or 1 pound fresh)

SAUCE

2 tablespoons ginger root, peeled and grated

2 cloves garlic, minced

1 tablespoon soy sauce

1 tablespoon oyster sauce

1 tablespoon rice vinegar

2 tablespoons Chinese rice wine or dry sherry

1½ tablespoons dark sesame oil

2 tablespoons fresh squeezed lime juice

1 tablespoon sugar

1 bunch green onions, finely chopped (keep white and green parts separate)

½ cup fat-free chicken stock

1 pound bay scallops

½ cup fresh cilantro, chopped

ADVANCE PREPARATION - 15 MINUTES

Make a sauce by combining ginger, garlic, soy sauce, oyster sauce, vinegar, wine, sesame oil, lime juice and sugar. Chop green onions as specified. (Chop cilantro at the last minute.) **Ingredients**

WINE PICK
Riesling

may be prepared <u>up to 8 hours in</u> <u>advance</u> if refrigerated.

FINAL PREPARATION - 15 MINUTES

1. Combine white part of green onions with chicken stock in a large stir-fry pan or skillet. Cook over medium heat until green onions are soft, about 5 minutes. Stir in sauce mixture and bring to a simmer. Add scallops and cook until opaque, about 2–3 minutes only. Be careful not to overcook scallops!

2. Meanwhile, cook pasta in plenty of rapidly boiling salted water until *al dente*. Drain and add directly to the sauce. Add cilantro and remaining green onions and toss thoroughly to combine. Serve immediately straight from the pan.

Jeanne Jones

TIPS, HINTS & SHORT-CUTS

For a vegetarian entree, use cubed firm tofu and substitute vegetable stock for the chicken stock. If you like spicy food, add ½ teaspoon (or to taste) of Chinese chili paste to the sauce.

NUTRITION DATA
(per serving)

*Calories: **505***

*Calories from Fat: **13.8%***

*Total Fat: **7.5 g***

*Saturated Fat: **1.0 g***

*Cholesterol: **38 mg***

*Sodium: **629 mg***

*Carbohydrates: **74 g***

*Dietary Fiber: **2.5 g***

*Protein: **14 g***

77

Pasta with Blackened Fish & Caper Salsa

Serves 4

This dish was inspired by a simple fresh tomato and caper sauce from the Tunisian islands of Kerkennah. Located on the North African side of the Mediterranean, cooks here traditionally use this salsa-like condiment as a topping for seafood. This recipes improves on a good thing by tossing the salsa with piping hot pasta and then topping the entire preparation with blackened fish. This recipe can also be made vegetarian-style by simply eliminating the fish.

WINE PICK
Pinot Grigio

PASTA
angel hair or thin pasta of your choice (¾ pound dried or 1 pound fresh)

SAUCE
1 tablespoon fresh squeezed lemon juice
1 tablespoon garlic, minced (divided use)
2 tablespoons Italian parsley, minced (divided use)
2 tablespoons olive oil (divided use)
1 pound red snapper, mahi mahi or orange roughy fillets, cut into 1" pieces
2 large tomatoes, peeled, seeded and coarsely chopped
1½ tablespoons capers, plus 1 tablespoon caper "juice" (the vinegar brine the capers are packed in)
¼ teaspoon salt
black pepper, to taste

ADVANCE PREPARATION - 30 MINUTES
Mix together lemon juice, ½ tablespoon garlic, 1 tablespoon parsley and 1 tablespoon olive oil. Pour into a plastic zipper lock freezer bag and add fish. Seal, shake to coat fish and marinate up to 4 hours in the refrigerator. Prepare tomatoes as specified and place in a colander to drain. Once thoroughly drained, make a

78

salsa by combining drained tomatoes,
capers, caper juice, salt, pepper, and
remaining garlic, parsley and olive oil.
Ingredients may be prepared <u>up to 4</u>
<u>hours in advance</u> if refrigerated.

FINAL PREPARATION - 20 MINUTES

1. Heat a heavy cast iron frying pan on
high heat for 10 minutes. (See Tips) While
pan heats, cook pasta in plenty of rapidly
boiling salted water until *al dente*. Drain,
toss with the salsa, and return to the same
(now empty) pot in which it was cooked.
This will keep the pasta hot for a few
minutes while the fish cooks.

2. Once the cast iron pan is hot enough,
cook the fish, letting it blacken on all sides.
This will only take 2–3 minutes! To test if
the pan is hot enough, scatter a few water
droplets on the hot surface. They should
"dance" for a few seconds before
evaporating. If they don't dance, the pan
still isn't hot enough. 1 minute before fish is
done, portion out pasta onto 4 pre-warmed
plates. Top with fish and serve immediately
while piping hot.

Kitty Morse

TIPS, HINTS &
SHORT-CUTS

<u>Blackening</u> is a
technique where food is
cooked over very intense
heat for a very short time.
Cooked this way, the
food's surface quickly
forms a blackened crust
which seals in natural
juices. You must use a
heavy cast iron skillet
because regular skillets
can't withstand or retain
the intense heat necessary
for effective blackening.
And make sure not to add
any oil—it will create
billows of smoke and
eventually ignite.

NUTRITION DATA
(per serving)

*Calories: **508***
*Calories from Fat: **17.7%***
*Total Fat: **9.9 g***
*Saturated Fat: **1.5 g***
*Cholesterol: **42 mg***
*Sodium: **248 mg***
*Carbohydrates: **68 g***
*Dietary Fiber: **2.9 g***
*Protein: **35 g***

Spaghetti with Garlic & Wilted Spinach

Serves 4–6

This is an adaptation of a recipe created for a contest by Henry Fenwick—one of Erica's original customers. (See Introduction) I must confess, however, that when we first received his entry, we were reluctant to try it. Quite frankly, the ingredients seemed like they would be better off in a Caesar salad! We tried it anyway and it instantly become one of our all-time favorites! In the coming years we made it often, experimenting with different methods and quantities each time. What follows is our favorite version. (And for anyone who's a little hesitant about the anchovies—relax! While they're an integral part of the dish, they don't make it taste "fishy!")

WINE PICK
Pinot Grigio

PASTA
spaghetti, linguine or pasta of your choice (1 pound dried or 1¼ pounds fresh)

SAUCE
1½ tablespoons olive oil
12 cloves garlic, minced
12 canned anchovy fillets, chopped
¼ cup capers (not rinsed)
splash of dry white wine or water
3 bunches fresh spinach, stems removed
¼ cup freshly grated Parmesan

ADVANCE PREPARATION - 10 MINUTES
Thoroughly clean spinach. (Or use pre-washed bagged spinach leaves.) If using baby spinach, keep leaves whole. If using regular spinach, tear leaves into halves or thirds. **Ingredients may be prepared <u>up to 8 hours in advance</u> if refrigerated.**

FINAL PREPARATION - 15 MINUTES
1. Heat olive oil in a large kettle over medium heat. Add garlic and sauté until golden. Add anchovies and, using a wooden spoon, simultaneously stir and mash them until they "dissolve" into the oil.

2. Add capers and cook 1 minute longer, stirring constantly.

3. Add spinach, tossing continuously until it wilts. Add a splash of wine or water to deglaze the kettle and to prevent the spinach from sticking. Reduce heat to low and keep warm.

4. Meanwhile, cook pasta in plenty of rapidly boiling salted water until *al dente*. Drain and add directly to spinach mixture. Toss gently to thoroughly entangle spinach with pasta. Serve straight from the kettle. Sprinkle Parmesan over each serving at the table.

Henry Fenwick
(Adapted by Chris Gluck)

TIPS, HINTS & SHORT-CUTS

Since spinach quickly wilts to a fraction of its original size when heated, seemingly large quantities are required initially. When served with pasta, spinach can be wilted either by adding it directly to the sauce along with all of the other ingredients (like this recipe), or by tossing it with freshly sauced hot pasta and letting the heat from the pasta do the wilting (like the recipe on page 32). Either way it's delicious!

NUTRITION DATA

(per serving)

*Calories: **417***
*Calories from Fat: **15.9%***
*Total Fat: **7.3 g***
*Saturated Fat: **1.8 g***
*Cholesterol: **6 mg***
*Sodium: **180 mg***
*Carbohydrates: **72 g***
*Dietary Fiber: **3.2 g***
*Protein: **16 g***

Pasta with Flambéed Shrimp

Serves 6

PASTA

linguine, fettuccine or pasta of your choice
(1 pound dried or 1¼ pounds fresh)

SAUCE

1 tablespoon olive oil

1 pound medium-sized raw shrimp, peeled and deveined

6 cloves garlic, minced

2 jalapeño peppers, seeded and finely diced

4 Roma tomatoes, diced

4 carrots, julienned and blanched

½ pound asparagus, cut into 1" pieces and blanched

1 cup gold tequila

1 cup fresh cilantro, chopped

3 limes, cut in half

ADVANCE PREPARATION - 30 MINUTES

Peel and devein shrimp. Prepare vegetables as specified. (Chop cilantro at the last minute.) **Ingredients may be prepared <u>up to 8 hours in advance</u> if refrigerated.**

WINE PICK
Chardonnay

FINAL PREPARATION - 15 MINUTES

1. Pre-heat a large kettle on high heat. Add olive oil. When oil is hot, add shrimp

and cook for a few seconds on each side. Add garlic and peppers and sauté 1 minute. Add tomatoes, carrots and asparagus and sauté 2 minutes longer.

2. Warm tequila in a small saucepan. Ignite. (See Tips) Immediately pour flaming tequila into kettle. When flame dies, add ½ cup water. Lower heat, season with salt and pepper if desired, and simmer 2 minutes.

3. Meanwhile, cook pasta in plenty of rapidly boiling salted water until *al dente*. Drain and immediately add cooked pasta directly to the sauce. Add cilantro, toss thoroughly and serve straight from the kettle. Squeeze ½ lime over each serving at the table.

Habib Kolahi

NUTRITION DATA
(per serving)

*Calories: **530***
*Calories from Fat: **10.7%***
*Total Fat: **5.4 g***
*Saturated Fat: **0.8 g***
*Cholesterol: **115 mg***
*Sodium: **143 mg***
*Carbohydrates: **72 g***
*Dietary Fiber: **5.7 g***
*Protein: **28 g***

Linguine with Mussels & Calamari

Serves 4–6

PASTA

linguine, fettuccine or pasta of your choice (¾ pound dried or 1 pound fresh)

SAUCE

6 cloves garlic, minced

1 yellow onion, chopped

2 cups fat-free chicken stock

1 pound baby calamari, cleaned and sliced into ¼" rings (or see substitutions in step #1)

4 Roma tomatoes, chopped

juice from 1 lemon

¼ cup fresh basil, chopped

¼ cup fresh cilantro, chopped

2 pounds mussels, well scrubbed

2 tablespoons cornstarch mixed with ¼ cup water

½ –1 teaspoon red pepper flakes

freshly ground black pepper, to taste

4 lemon wedges

ADVANCE PREPARATION - 45 MINUTES

Prepare vegetables as specified. (Chop fresh herbs at the last minute.) Clean and prepare calamari as specified. (See Tips) Clean mussels as specified. (See Tips on page 75.) **Ingredients may be prepared up to 8 hours in advance if refrigerated.**

WINE PICK
Chardonnay

Final Preparation - 20 minutes

1. Pre-heat a kettle on high heat. Add garlic, onions and chicken stock. Bring to a boil, then reduce heat and simmer 3 minutes. Add calamari and simmer 2 minutes longer. (If calamari is not available, substitute shrimp, slipper lobster tails, clams or more mussels.)

2. Add tomatoes, lemon juice, basil, cilantro and mussels. Cover and simmer until mussels open, about 5 minutes.

3. Add cornstarch mixture and pepper flakes to taste. Stir well and keep warm on lowest heat.

4. Meanwhile, cook pasta in plenty of rapidly boiling salted water until *al dente*. Drain and divide among 4–6 large pre-heated plates. Portion out seafood on top of pasta and pour sauce over each serving. Top with freshly ground black pepper and garnish with lemon wedges. Serve immediately.

Joseph Savino

Tips, Hints & Short-Cuts

*To **clean and prepare baby calamari**: 1) Pull off and discard the head and tentacles, 2) Pull out the transparent quill-like bone, 3) Peel off the purple skin, 4) Thoroughly clean and rinse the interior of the body sac, 5) Slice the body sac crosswise into rings. (Or, if you're not up to this somewhat tedious task, cheat and buy frozen calamari—already cleaned and sliced into rings!)*

Nutrition Data
(per serving)

*Calories: **557***
*Calories from Fat: **11.3%***
*Total Fat: **6.9 g***
*Saturated Fat: **1.3 g***
*Cholesterol: **264 mg***
*Sodium: **910 mg***
*Carbohydrates: **74 g***
*Dietary Fiber: **3.3 g***
*Protein: **47 g***

Glossary

Al dente Italian for "to the tooth." It means to cook pasta until it's tender but still firm.

Angel hair Very thin, round pasta strands.

Bean thread noodles A semi-transparent type of Asian pasta made from mung bean starch. See Tips on page 71 for more information.

Blackening A cooking technique where food is cooked in a cast iron skillet over very intense heat for a very short time. See Tips on page 79 for more information.

Blanch To briefly plunge food into boiling water and then to immediately rinse in cold water. In addition to slightly pre-cooking food, blanching also helps preserve color and flavor, especially in green vegetables and herbs.

Capers The unopened floral bud of a wild Mediterranean shrub. Typically packed in a salty vinegar brine which helps preserve them and reduces their bitterness. Use sparingly—a few go a long way.

Caramelizing A cooking technique similar to "French frying." Food is cooked in oil so hot that it creates a crispy "skin" which stops the oil from being absorbed and seals in natural juices. See Tips on page 33 for more information.

Chiffonade To slice leafy herbs or vegetables into very fine strips. See Tips on page 27 for more information.

Chinese chili paste An extremely hot blend of pureed fresh and dried chiles mixed with vinegar and sometimes other ingredients. Readily available in the international section of most supermarkets.

Chipotles en adobo Dried, smoked red jalapeño peppers that are packed in adobo, a vinegar-based sauce of tomatoes, onions and garlic. For convenience and ease of measuring, puree chipotles and the adobo sauce together in a blender. It will keep at least a year if refrigerated. Available in well-stocked supermarkets, specialty stores and ethnic markets. There is no substitute for their intense, complex, smoky flavor.

Conchiglie Small pasta shells.

Deglaze The process of releasing the bits of food that caramelize or stick to the bottom of a pan during roasting or sautéing. Adding a liquid (typically stock, juice, wine, spirits or water) to the hot pan dissolves these pan deposits and releases their concentrated flavors. See Tips on page 69 for more information.

Devein To remove the dark vein from shrimp. Most effectively done by using an inexpensive shrimp deveining tool that cuts through the shell, makes the incision and cuts out the vein in one fell swoop. Although somewhat more tedious, it can also be done by cutting a shallow incision along the outside edge of a peeled raw shrimp with a sharp paring knife and then pulling or scraping out the vein by hand.

Farfalle Small, bow tie-shaped pasta.

Fettuccine Flat pasta strands approximately ¼" wide.

Fusilli Short, twisted or spiral-shaped pasta.

Ginger root Not really a root, but an underground stem, or rhizome. Although hot and spicy, it has the unique ability to simultaneously cool and heat the palate. Readily available year round in the produce section of all grocery stores. Peel first, then grate, mince or finely slice against the grain. Do not confuse with powdered ginger found in the spice section.

Gnocchi Tiny Italian potato dumplings about the size of a large garlic clove. Readily available in most supermarkets in shelf-stable, vacuum-packed packages, or individually quick frozen in the freezer section. Cook in boiling water just until they float; then retrieve with a slotted spoon. Can also be stir-fried after boiling. See recipe and Tips on page 45 for more information.

Greek olives (see Kalamata olives)

Julienne To cut food into pieces about the size of match sticks.

Kalamata olives Ripe olives that have been cured in a salt brine to which vinegar has been added upon packing. Readily available canned in all supermarkets or in bulk in ethnic (Italian or Middle Eastern) markets and delicatessens.

Liquid smoke A concentrated smoke seasoning. Can be used in marinades or sparingly added directly to sauces, soups or meats. Readily available in the condiment section of all supermarkets.

Linguine Flat, thin pasta strands.

Oil-cured black olives Rich, strong-flavored black olives covered with a thin film of oil. Sold loose, not packed in brine. Available in jars in most well-stocked supermarkets or in bulk in ethnic (Italian or Middle Eastern) markets and delicatessens.

Oyster sauce A thick, smoky yet sweet Asian sauce. Readily available in the international section of all supermarkets.

Penne Short, tube-shaped pasta approximately 3/8" in diameter.

Radiatore Small pasta with protruding wavy, radiator-like fins. Approximately 1" in diameter.

Red chile powder Pure ground dried chiles. Available in many different varieties from mild to hot. The milder types found in most supermarkets are perfect for the recipes in this book. Do not confuse with commercial chile powder which is typically a blend of ground chile mixed with cumin and garlic.

Reduce The process of heating a liquid until a portion of it evaporates, leaving behind a richer, more concentrated liquid. See Tips on page 69 for more information.

Rice vinegar   A mild, almost sweet, low acid type of Asian vinegar.   Use sparingly in sauces or marinades.   Readily available in the international section of most supermarkets.

Roasting Peppers (How to)   Grill or broil bell peppers or chiles until the skins char.   Immediately put them in a large bowl tightly sealed with plastic wrap.   This will cause the peppers to "sweat," making them easier to peel.   Peel off the skins when the peppers are cool enough to handle, taking care to reserve the flavorful juices.   Never peel peppers under running water!   Even though this will make the process go faster, it will also wash away much of the flavor.

Sesame oil   A dark, nutty-tasting oil pressed from toasted sesame seeds.   Unusual in that it is used only for flavoring—not for cooking.   Readily available in the international section of most supermarkets.

Shiitake mushrooms   A rich, meaty-flavored mushroom.   Stem is inedible.   Readily available fresh in the produce section of most supermarkets, or dehydrated in Asian markets.

Spaghetti   Thin, round pasta strands.

Spaghettini   See angel hair.

Sweat   To slowly cook food over low heat in a small amount of low-fat or fat-free liquid (typically water, stock or juice) until soft.   Sometimes a small amount of olive oil or other fat is added to the liquid to hasten the cooking process and prevent initial sticking.

Zest   The thin outer layer of citrus fruit.   See Tips on page 35 for more information.

Index

91

PastaPress.com

Visit Our Website For More Great Low-Fat Pasta Recipes!

Praise for Pasta Press Magazine

"Flavor meets health."

Albuquerque Journal

"There have been a lot of food magazines, but few with as clear a focus as Pasta Press. This is a clear, no-nonsense, attractive publication."

Los Angeles Times

"Handsomely organized and illustrated."

Hartford Courant

"Offers lots of recipes, cooking tips, resources and lore in a lively, user-friendly format."

Asbury Park Press

"One of the neatest food magazines we've seen in a long time. Crammed with easy-to-follow instructions, good natured cooking tips, and fetching illustrations."

Seattle Times

"Innovative recipes, and all under 20% of calories from fat."

Dayton News

"Bright look and sensible format makes it a welcome addition for pasta lovers."

Tulsa World

"All of the recipes can be made by the average cook."

Portland Oregonian

Also by Chris Gluck

Pasta & Vegetables: Low-Fat Recipes…That Work!

PastaPress.com

Visit Our Website For More Great Low-Fat Pasta Recipes!